200

New Food Combining Recipes

*Tasty Dishes from Around
the World*

INGE DRIES

ELEMENT

Shaftesbury, Dorset • Rockport, Massachusetts
Brisbane, Queensland

First published in Dutch under the title *200 Heerlijke gerechten*

© Arinus 1993

Published in Great Britain in 1995 by
Element Books Limited
Shaftesbury, Dorset

Published in the USA in 1995 by
Element, Inc.
42 Broadway, Rockport, MA 01966

Published in Australia in 1995 by
Element Books Limited
for Jacaranda Wiley Limited
33 Park Road, Milton, Brisbane 4064

Cover illustration Guy Ryecart
Cover design by The Bridgewater Book Company
Design by Roger Lightfoot
Illustrations by Mary Stubberfield
Typeset by Phil Payter Graphics
Printed and bound in Great Britain by
Biddles Ltd, Guildford & King's Lynn

British Library Cataloguing in Publication data available

Library of Congress Cataloging in Publication data available

ISBN 1–85230–579–7

200 New Food Combining Recipes

Inge Dries grew up in a family where the attention was focused on healthy food and a natural way of life. From her mother, she inherited the love for preparing food and her father taught her everything about dietary rules. As a graphic designer, she pays a lot of attention to the presentation of her dishes, all of which are composed according to the correct food combinations. With these 200 tasty dishes, Inge Dries helps the reader apply the food combinations in a simple and pleasant way.

Contents

Introduction

Many people suffer acutely from problems of digestion. Acid indigestion, heartburn, wind in the stomach, intestinal flatulence, food lying heavy on the stomach after a meal – all these are widespread complaints. They are so common that people tend to take them for granted, and carry indigestion tablets or powders around with them in case such problems become too pressing. But these precautionary measures do not actually treat the root cause.

All too few people know that digestive problems inevitably follow the consumption of types of food that should not be eaten together. The discomforts of indigestion arise after eating foods that should not be combined within the human digestive system. In time, the combining of such badly matched foods can lead to disease.

In addition to immediate problems of digestion, the combining of the wrong foods may be associated with a number of other ailments that at first sight seem to have little or no connection. A closer study shows, however, that such disorders as nutritional deficiency through the malabsorption of nutrients, some food allergies, breathlessness, and palpitations of the heart – among others – are inextricably bound up with a digestive system that for one reason or another is in poor shape. The fermentation and toxic degradation of food within the stomach is a theme of popular debate among gastroenterologists.

Every food is made up of nutrients, which are metabolized by the body to provide heat energy (measured in kilocalories or kilojoules). The three major forms of nutrient are protein (P), fats (F) and carbohydrates which, for the purposes of this book, are distinguished as starch (St) and sugars (Su) because they have different effects on food combining. Acids (A) also supply

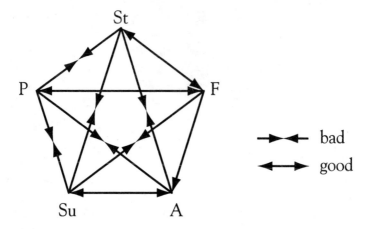

The Food Combining Diagram

heat energy, but are only minimally present, and so are generally ignored. They are, however, very significant to food combining, and therefore have to be included as a nutrient in their own right. In total, then, there are five forms of nutrient that have to be taken into account when considering food combining.

The five may be represented in the form of a pentagon, which constitutes not only a symbol for food combining but a very practical means of becoming familiar with the combinations of foods involved.

Most important of all is to remember which combinations of food nutrients go well together (are good combinations) and which combinations of food nutrients react badly with each other (are bad combinations). They are:

good	bad
protein + fat	protein + starch
fat + starch	protein + sugar
fat + acid	sugar + fat
sugar + acid	starch + acid
	starch + sugar
	acid + protein

The Dominant Nutrient

One comment often made is that there are four or five nutrients present in everything we eat: we therefore cannot help but eat all these nutrients at the same time. Even if we stick always to eating only a single type of food, we are bound to eat four or five nutrients together. The comment is well founded. Certainly there are four or five nutrients present in everything we eat – but not in the same proportion. Only one of the nutrients has a dominant effect, usually by being present in larger proportion. It is the dominant nutrient that is highly significant to food combining, therefore.

beef steak

P: 19 %
F: 5 %

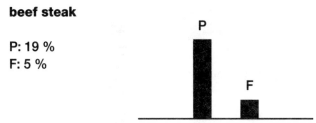

In beef steak, protein is dominant. There is not much fat, and very little in the way of carbohydrates.

avocado

P: 2 %
→F: 24 %
St/Su: 1 %

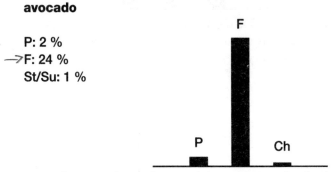

Avocado is mostly made up of fat. Fat is evidently the dominant nutrient.

whole-grain rice

P: 7 %
F: 2 %
St: 75 %

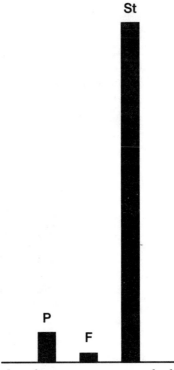

In whole-grain rice, starch is dominant – as it is indeed in all cereal products and in all foods that contain grain, such as bread, waffles, pasta and many other everyday foods.

banana

Su

P: 1 %
F: 0.2 %
Su: 22 %

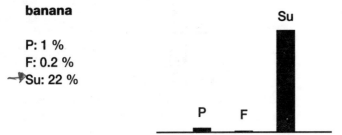

Sugar is evidently the dominant nutrient in this food: the content of fat and protein is negligible.

lemon

P: 1 %
F: 0.5 %
Su: 8 %
A: 5 %

Acid is the dominant nutrient in a lemon – although the sugar content is proportionately greater.

It is a quirk of nature that in some foods – notably leguminous vegetables – protein and starch have the same degree of dominance. Legumes are for this very reason generally difficult to digest.

These examples demonstrate the great difference between eating a single type of food all the time and eating a great variety of foods at random. The proportion of the dominant nutrient in each food is highly significant, as is the total quantity eaten. Specifically, it is obvious that if we eat a combination of foods, the dominant nutrient in each must be compatible with the others. This is the heart of food combining – to achieve nutritional harmony and enjoy optimal digestion.

Through food combining it is possible to eat several types of food in one meal and still have no problems whatever with digestion. Human evolution, however, goes back to a time when it was normal for humans to eat only one type of food (as, after all, most animals still do): it is actually more natural for humans to eat only a single type of food, at least at any one meal.

Since then, of course, we have become 'civilized'. We eat other types of food, notably agricultural produce, and we prepare it by cooking it or by doing other things to it. In effect, we have taken up using combinations of foods that are bad for us simply as a matter of cultural 'progress'. Agricultural produce is not always suited to human consumption – which is why it often has to be processed in one way or another. The processing may in turn give it an unpleasant taste, and for that reason agricultural produce is generally used together with other forms of food.

Humans have strayed from the single fare that was natural to them, and the food industry (historically and now) has been largely responsible for forcing the pace of that dietary change. Today, food products are processed in whatever way takes the least time, and conversely, many people have no time to eat anything but fast-food. Human digestive physiology is simply not taken into account. People do not ask themselves whether their digestive system is capable of dealing with what they throw at it. Despite the cultural evolution in eating habits that has been taking place over the millennia, the human digestive system has not itself changed in any meaningful way.

To profit from eating combinations of foods that genuinely go well together, it is necessary to have some idea of the dominant nutrients in each of the various foods we eat. Much of the hard work has already been done for you, in this case, for the principles of food combining have been fully incorporated in the following recipes.

If you would like to learn more about the theory of food combining, Jan Dries' *The New Book of Food Combining* shows how simple dietary changes can improve health and well-being and help overcome digestive problems.

Using these recipes, you will become familiar with the types of food and the combinations of food that are good for you and which will bring relief to your digestive system, and thereby improve your overall health. You will find, in addition, that you are eating food that is delicious and truly good for you at the same time.

		acids					starch			sugar		fat			protein		
Category	**Food**	mushrooms	milk	vegetables	vegetables (lactic acid)	yoghurt – butter milk	tomato	vinegar – mustard	fruits – berries	vegetables rich in starch	potato	cereals – bread – pasta	fruit rich in sugar	sugar – honey	avocado – olive	butter – whipped cream	oil – fat – egg yolk	nuts – seeds – pips	cheese – cottage cheese	meat – fish – poultry
protein	meat – fish – poultry	✓	–	✓	–	–	✓	–	–	×	–	–	–	–	–	–	–	–	–	■
	cheese – cottage cheese	✓	–	✓	–	×	✓	–	✓	×	–	–	–	–	–	–	–	–	■	–
	nuts – seeds – pips	•	–	✓	✓	×	✓	–	✓	×	–	–	–	–	–	–	–	■	–	–
fat	oil – fat – egg yolk	✓	×	✓	✓	✓	✓	✓	✓	✓	✓	✓	×	–	–	–	■	–	–	–
	butter – whipped cream	✓	×	✓	✓	✓	✓	✓	✓	✓	✓	✓	×	–	–	■	–	–	–	–
	avocado – olive	✓	–	✓	✓	✓	✓	✓	✓	✓	✓	✓	–	–	■	–	–	–	–	–
sugar	sugar – honey	–	–	–	–	✓	•	•	✓	×	–	–	×	■	–	–	–	–	–	–
	fruit rich in sugar	–	–	–	–	✓	–	×	✓	×	–	–	■	×	–	×	×	–	–	–
starch	cereals – bread – pasta	✓	–	✓	–	–	–	–	–	✓	✓	■	–	–	✓	✓	✓	–	–	–
	potato	✓	–	✓	–	–	–	–	–	✓	■	✓	–	–	✓	✓	✓	–	–	–
	vegetables rich in starch	✓	–	✓	✓	✓	×	×	×	■	✓	✓	×	×	✓	✓	✓	×	×	×
acids	fruits – berries	–	×	×	×	✓	×	✓	■	×	–	–	✓	✓	✓	✓	✓	✓	✓	✓
	vinegar – mustard	✓	×	✓	×	–	✓	■	✓	×	–	–	×	•	✓	✓	✓	–	–	–
	tomato	✓	×	✓	✓	✓	■	✓	×	×	–	–	–	•	✓	✓	✓	✓	✓	✓
	yoghurt – butter milk	•	✓	✓	✓	■	✓	–	✓	✓	–	–	✓	✓	✓	✓	✓	✓	×	×
	vegetables (lactic acid)	✓	×	✓	■	✓	✓	×	×	✓	–	–	–	–	–	✓	✓	✓	–	–
	vegetables	✓	×	■	✓	✓	✓	✓	×	✓	✓	✓	–	–	✓	✓	✓	✓	✓	✓
	milk	•	■	×	×	✓	×	×	×	–	–	–	–	–	–	×	×	–	–	–
	mushrooms	■	•	✓	✓	•	✓	✓	–	✓	✓	✓	–	–	✓	✓	✓	•	✓	✓

✓ good combinations   × difficult combinations
– bad combinations   • good, but not usual

The Food Combining Chart

Before You Start . . .

The recipes in this book give quantities in metric and Imperial measures. Remember to follow only one set of measures in a recipe: they are not interchangeable.

These recipes refer to Imperial **pints**, as used in the UK and Australia. An Imperial pint contains 20 fl oz, whereas the US pint is 16 fl oz.

Where quantities are given in **cups**, they refer to the US 8 fl oz measuring cup.

Throughout this book, **tablespoons** refer to the UK standard. This holds 17.7 ml. The US tablespoon holds 14.2 ml and the Australian 20 ml. (A teaspoon is standard at approximately 5 ml.) The table below gives a conversion chart for reference when multiples of tablespoons are required.

British	American	Australian
1 teaspoon	1 teaspoon	1 teaspoon
1 tablespoon	1 tablespoon	1 tablespoon
2 tablespoons	3 tablespoons	2 tablespoons
3½ tablespoons	4 tablespoons	3 tablespoons
4 tablespoons	5 tablespoons	3½ tablespoons

Appetizers

Stuffed Mushrooms
(serves 4)

20 large mushrooms
1 shallot
1 tbsp butter
1 garlic clove
3 basil leaves
1 parsley sprig
chives
pepper
breadcrumbs
butter
mixed salad

1. Rub the mushrooms clean. (Never wash mushrooms as they absorb water and become spongy.) Remove the stalks and chop finely.
2. Peel the shallot, chop finely and sauté in the butter together with the finely chopped mushroom stalks and garlic.
3. Wash the basil, parsley and chives, pat dry and chop finely. Add the herbs to the mushroom mixture and season with pepper.
4. Fill the mushroom buttons with the mixture and sprinkle with some breadcrumbs.
5. Place some butter on each mushroom and grill until golden brown.
6. Serve on a bed of mixed salad.

(See also recipe on p. 106.)

Southern Tomatoes
(serves 4)

4 small tomatoes
1 or 2 mozzarella cheeses
4 crinkly lettuce leaves
12 basil leaves

1. Wash the tomatoes, remove the stems and slice.
2. Slice the mozzarella cheese using an egg slicer.
3. Arrange alternate slices of cheese and tomato on top of a lettuce leaf on each of 4 dessert plates.
4. Garnish the salad with basil.

Avocado Stuffed with Raw Vegetables

(serves 4)

2 ripe avocados
1 tbsp lemon juice
4 red lettuce leaves
4 mushrooms
¼ peeled cucumber
4 radishes
1 tbsp oil
½ tbsp lemon juice
fresh herbs

1. Cut the avocados in half, remove the stones and sprinkle the flesh of the fruit with lemon juice to prevent discoloration.
2. Wash the lettuce, pat dry, cut in strips and fill the hollow of the avocado with these strips.
3. Rub the mushrooms clean and slice thinly. Slice the cucumber thinly.
4. Fill the avocado halves with the mushroom and cucumber slices.
5. Garnish with the radishes and pour the dressing consisting of oil, lemon juice and herbs over it.

Spicy Mushroom Slices

(serves 4)

4 slices of bread
herb mayonnaise
  (see p. 115 for
  recipe)
4 lettuce leaves
100 g (4 oz)
  mushrooms
lemon juice
fresh herbs

1. Toast the bread.
2. Spread the toast with the herb mayonnaise.
3. Wash the lettuce, pat dry, cut into strips and place on the toast.
4. Rub the mushrooms clean, slice thinly and arrange on top of the lettuce.
5. Sprinkle with lemon juice and garnish with fresh, finely chopped herbs.

Scrambled Eggs with Fresh Herbs

(serves 4)

4 brown eggs
2 tbsp fresh chopped herbs
1 tbsp oil
chives

1. Take the eggs and carefully crack the shell at the smaller end. (The shells are needed later in the recipe.) Pour the contents of the eggs into a bowl and whisk until frothy.
2. Blend the herbs with the eggs.
3. Heat the oil, add the eggs and allow to set while stirring constantly.
4. Carefully rinse the eggshells with water and fill them with the scrambled eggs. Place the eggs in 4 attractive egg-cups (preferably with a high base) and garnish with a few blades of chives.

Garlic Tomatoes

(serves 4)

1 small bowl cherry tomatoes
a few leaves of lettuce
3 parsley sprigs
3 basil leaves
1 garlic clove
1 tbsp oil

1. Wash the tomatoes, dry and remove the stems.
2. Wash the parsley and basil, dry and chop finely. Peel the garlic and chop finely.
3. Heat the oil and sauté the tomatoes, sprinkling the garlic and herbs onto them.
4. Serve the tomatoes on a bed of lettuce.

Stuffed Artichoke

(serves 4)

4 medium-sized
  globe artichokes
3 tbsp mayonnaise
1 tbsp yoghurt
2 tbsp fresh herbs,
  chopped
2 pickled gherkins
1 shallot
pepper
paprika
salt

1. Thoroughly wash the artichokes, cut the stalks and cook in a saucepan of water. An artichoke is ready when its base can be pierced with a fork. Take the artichokes out of the water and let them cool.
2. Remove the middle part (the small leaves) from the artichokes, making the heart visible. Remove the hearts and cut off pieces at the bottom, so that the artichokes will stand up.
3. Blend the mayonnaise, yoghurt and herbs.
4. Finely chop the gherkins. Peel the shallot and slice thinly. Blend both into the sauce.
5. Season the sauce with pepper, paprika and salt.

6. Fill the hollow of the artichokes with the sauce and serve. Peel off the leaves of the artichoke one by one and dip them in the sauce. The lower part of each leaf is edible, the rest is not. After you have eaten the leaves and finished the sauce, you will find the delicious base.

Oyster Mushrooms Coated with Breadcrumbs

(serves 4)

400 g (14 oz) small oyster mushrooms
1 egg white
3 or 4 tbsp breadcrumbs and/or sesame seeds
oil or butter

1. Wipe the mushrooms (do not wash).
2. Beat the egg white and pour into a soup plate.
3. Put the breadcrumbs or sesame seeds onto 1 or 2 plates.
4. First, dip the mushrooms in the egg white, then in the breadcrumbs and/or the sesame seeds.
5. Fry the mushrooms in the oil or butter until they are golden brown.

Fennel au Gratin

(serves 4)

2 fennel roots
pepper
paprika
4 slices Camembert cheese
curly endive

1. Cut the fennel roots in half, wash and cook or steam.
2. Put the halved fennel roots in a greased, heat-resistant oven dish and sprinkle with pepper and paprika.
3. Place the Camembert over the fennel and grill.
4. Serve on 4 plates, garnished with the endive.

Avocado Dip
(serves 4)

2 avocados
1 tbsp lemon juice
4 radishes
3 basil leaves
lettuce
tacos

1. Cut the avocados in half, remove the stones and scoop out the flesh with a teaspoon. (The shells will be needed later in the recipe.)
2. Purée the flesh in a blender until smooth. Add lemon juice to prevent discoloration.
3. Wash the radishes, dry and slice thinly.
4. Fill the hollow shells with the avocado purée and garnish with the radish slices.
5. Wash the basil, pat dry, shred finely and sprinkle onto the avocados.
6. Serve the avocados halves on 4 small plates with lettuce and warm tacos.

Tasty Croissants
(serves 4)

3 or 4 (frozen) squares of puff pastry
6 mushrooms
garlic
pepper
fresh herbs
2 sautéed shallots
3 tbsp fried vegetables (onions, carrots, broccoli, etc.)

1. Defrost the pastry 15 minutes before it is needed.
2. Cut each square diagonally to form 4 triangles.
3. Rub the mushrooms clean, slice and sauté adding a little garlic and pepper.
4. Fill ⅓ of the triangles with the mushroom mixture and roll into croissants. Fill ½ of the remaining pastry with fresh herbs and sautéed shallot.
5. Fill the rest of the pastry with fried vegetables.
6. Bake the croissants in a preheated oven for 10 to 15 minutes.

Easter Egg Nests
(serves 4)

½ head of lettuce
3 eggs
12 cherry tomatoes
herb mayonnaise
  (see p. 115 for
  recipe)

1. Wash the lettuce, dry and cut into strips. Form a 'nest' of lettuce on 4 plates.
2. Hard boil the eggs. Let them cool and cut lengthwise into 4 slices. Fill each nest with 3 slices of egg.
3. Wash the tomatoes, dry and divide among the nests.
4. Serve with herb mayonnaise.

Stuffed Eggs
(serves 4)

a few lettuce leaves
4 eggs
1 or 2 tbsp
  mayonnaise
1 tsp curry powder
mustard and cress

1. Wash the lettuce, dry and spread over 4 plates.
2. Hard boil the eggs. Let them cool and cut in half. Remove the egg yolks, mash and blend with the mayonnaise and curry powder.
3. Use a piping bag to fill the eggs with the yolk mixture. Arrange the stuffed eggs on the plates and garnish with mustard and cress.

Soups

Vegetable Stock

3 litres (7 pints;
  16 cups) water
1 celeriac
2 onions
1 carrot
2 leeks
pepper
1 tbsp salt
2 garlic cloves
2 bay leaves

For a quick stock use instant vegetable stock granules or bouillon powder, which can also be used for seasoning instead of salt. For homemade vegetable stock:
1. Clean the vegetables and cut into pieces.
2. Put the vegetables into a large pan of hot water with the pepper, salt, garlic and bay leaves.
3. Simmer with the lid on for 2 hours.
4. Strain the stock through a sieve and use as required. (The stock can be frozen and used later.)

Clear Vegetable Soup or Consommé
(serves 4)

1 large carrot
½ small celeriac
1 red pepper
1 small courgette
1 shallot
1 tbsp oil
1 litre (1¾ pints;
  4 cups) vegetable
  stock (see above for
  recipe)
parsley

1. Wash or peel the carrot and slice.
2. Peel the celeriac and cut into strips.
3. Wash the red pepper, remove the seeds and cut into strips.
4. Wash the courgette and use a small melon scoop to remove the seeds.
5. Thinly slice the shallot.
6. Heat the oil and sauté the shallot. Add the sliced vegetables and cook gently for a while. Add the stock and bring to the boil, making sure the soup does not boil for more than 2 minutes.
7. Serve with finely chopped parsley.

Raw Vegetable Soup
(serves 4)

1 carrot
½ shallot
½ small celeriac
¼ cucumber
1 litre (1¾ pints;
  4 cups) vegetable
  stock (see p. 10 for
  recipe)
parsley

1. Wash or peel the carrot.
2. Peel the shallot, celeriac and cucumber and cut into pieces.
3. Put the vegetables in a blender with the hot stock.
4. Garnish with finely chopped parsley. Serve hot or cold.

Creamy Cucumber Soup with Dill
(serves 4)

1 large cucumber
1 tbsp butter
2 tbsp flour
1 litre (1¾ pints;
  4 cups) vegetable
  stock (see p. 10 for
  recipe)
3 dill sprigs
cream

1. Peel the cucumber, cut into pieces and purée in a blender (add water if necessary).
2. Heat the butter in a pan and stir in the flour (creating a roux).
3. When the butter has absorbed the flour completely, add the stock stirring constantly. Add the cucumber purée and let the soup heat through until creamy, stirring occasionally.
4. Wash the dill, pat dry, chop finely and add just before serving. For a special occasion, add a splash of cream to the soup.

(This recipe can be used for converting all vegetables into a creamy soup.)

Gazpacho

(serves 4)

1 cucumber
1 red pepper
3 large beefsteak
tomatoes
1 shallot
½ tbsp olive oil
2 garlic cloves
parsley

1. Peel the cucumber.
2. Wash the red pepper and remove the seeds.
3. Skin the tomatoes and remove the seeds.
4. Peel the shallot.
5. Cut all the vegetables into pieces and put in a blender with the oil and garlic.
6. Serve cold and garnish with finely chopped pepper, cucumber and parsley if required.

Leek Soup

(serves 4)

3 leeks
1 tbsp butter or
margarine
1 tbsp flour
1 litre (1¾ pints;
4 cups) vegetable
stock (see p. 10 for
recipe)
pepper
1 tbsp fresh lemon
balm, chopped

1. Remove the dark green part from the leeks. Wash the rest thoroughly and slice into rings. Stew the leek in butter or margarine.
2. Heat the butter or margarine and stir in the flour.
3. When the butter has absorbed the flour completely, add the stock, stirring constantly. Add the leek and let the soup heat through for a few minutes.
4. Season the soup with pepper. Just before serving, add the lemon balm.

For a special occasion, stir in some cream.

Onion Soup
(serves 4)

4 large onions
2 potatoes
1 tbsp butter
1 litre (1¾ pints;
  4 cups) vegetable
  stock (see p. 10 for
  recipe)
2 bay leaves
chives
croûtons

1. Peel and finely chop the onions.
2. Peel the potatoes and cut into cubes.
3. Heat the butter and sauté the onions and the potatoes.
4. Add the stock and bay leaves.
5. Let the soup cook for 10 minutes, then blend if preferred.
6. Garnish with chives and croûtons if required.

Raw Tomato Soup
(serves 4)

3 tomatoes
½ cucumber
½ shallot
1 stick celery
1 litre (1¾ pints;
  4 cups) vegetable
  stock (see p. 10 for
  recipe)
fresh basil, chopped

1. Skin the tomatoes and remove the seeds.
2. Peel the cucumber and shallots, chop finely and put in a blender with the tomatoes.
3. Wash the celery, chop finely and blend with the other vegetables.
4. Meanwhile, boil the stock. Mix the vegetables with the hot stock and season with basil.
5. Serve the soup immediately.

Mushroom Soup

(serves 4)

250 g (9 oz)
  mushrooms
1 tbsp butter
1 tbsp flour
1 litre (1¾ pints;
  4 cups) vegetable
  stock (see p. 10 for
  recipe)
pepper
fresh parsley,
  chopped

1. Rub the mushrooms clean, slice and sauté in the butter.
2. Add the flour, while stirring constantly.
3. When the butter has absorbed the flour completely, add the stock.
4. Add the mushrooms and let the soup cook for a few minutes. Season the soup with pepper.
5. Garnish with parsley.

(This recipe can be used for turning all vegetables into a creamy soup.)

Clear Bouillon Soup
(serves 4)

1 carrot
100 g (4 oz)
  mushrooms
6 small cauliflower
  florets
1 leek
1 tbsp oil
1 litre (1¾ pints;
  4 cups) vegetable
  stock (see p. 10 for
  recipe)
1 tbsp soy sauce
pepper
lettuce leaves

1. Peel the carrot and cut into even slices of more or less 1 mm width.
2. Rub the mushrooms clean, remove the lower part of the stalks and slice.
3. Wash the cauliflower.
4. Wash the leek, remove any roots and green parts and slice into rings.
5. Heat the oil and sauté the vegetables in it for a short time only.
6. Add the stock and let the soup cook for no longer than 2 minutes in order to keep the vegetables crisp. Season with soy sauce.
7. Just before serving, arrange 2 lettuce leaves on each plate. Pour the broth over the lettuce and serve hot.

Cauliflower-Broccoli Soup
(serves 4)

½ small cauliflower
1 small broccoli head
1 shallot
1 carrot
1 tbsp oil
1 litre (1¾ pints;
  4 cups) vegetable
  stock (see p. 10 for
  recipe)
pepper
fresh herbs, chopped

1. Thoroughly wash the cauliflower and separate into florets.
2. Do the same with the broccoli.
3. Peel the shallot and carrot and cut finely.
4. Gently cook the vegetables in the oil for 2 minutes. Add the stock and let the soup simmer for 2 or 3 minutes only, so that the cauliflower and the broccoli remain crisp.
5. Season with pepper and garnish with fresh herbs.

Creamy Asparagus Soup

(serves 4)

---

1 bundle of
  asparagus
1 litre (1¾ pints;
  4 cups) vegetable
  stock (see p. 10 for
  recipe)
1 tbsp butter
1 tbsp flour
3 tbsp cream
fresh dill

1. Wash the asparagus, removing the fibrous lower part (but save it for the stock, together with the skins) and cut the asparagus into equal pieces.
2. Prepare a vegetable stock and add the asparagus skins and fibrous parts. Heat the butter and stir the flour into it.
3. When the butter has absorbed the flour completely, add the strained stock and asparagus pieces, but set aside the asparagus tips. Let the soup cook until the asparagus pieces are well done. 5 minutes before serving the soup, add the asparagus tips.
4. When the soup is ready, add the cream and garnish with dill.

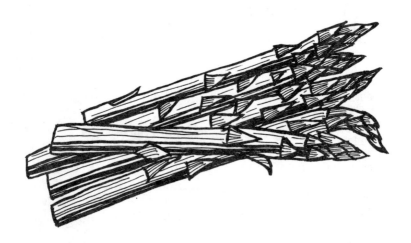

Festive Cream Soup

(serves 4)

---

1 leek
1 fennel root
1 celery stalk
1 shallot
1 carrot
1 tbsp butter
1 litre (1¾ pints;
 4 cups) vegetable
 stock (see p. 10 for
 recipe)
saffron
3 thyme sprigs
125 ml (¼ pint;
 ½ cup) cream

1. Clean (removing any roots and green parts), wash and shred the leek and fennel root.
2. Peel and shred the celery, shallot and carrot.
3. Heat the butter and cook the vegetables for a short time only.
4. Add the stock, saffron and thyme.
5. Bring the soup to the boil and let it cook for 5 to 10 minutes.
6. Just before serving, add the cream.

Celeriac Soup

(serves 4)

---

1 celeriac
1 large potato
2 carrots
1 onion
1 tbsp oil
1.5 litre (2½ pints;
 6 cups) vegetable
 stock (see p. 10 for
 recipe)
1 bay leaf
parsley

1. Peel and cut the celeriac, potato, carrots and onion into cubes.
2. Heat the oil and sauté the vegetables for a short time only.
3. Add the stock and let the soup cook until the vegetables are ready.
4. Put the soup in a blender and when smooth sprinkle with some parsley.

Avocado Soup

(serves 4)

2 avocados
1 litre (1¾ pints;
  4 cups) vegetable
  stock (see p. 10 for
  recipe)
pepper
fresh herbs

1. Peel the avocados, remove the stones and cut the flesh into pieces.
2. Meanwhile, boil the stock.
3. Add the avocado to the stock and transfer to a blender.
4. Season with pepper and garnish with fresh herbs.

Chinese Vegetable Soup

(serves 4)

2 spring onions
½ red pepper
150 g (5 oz)
  beansprouts
1 carrot
1 tbsp oil
1 tbsp soy sauce
1 litre (1¾ pints;
  4 cups) cold
  vegetable stock
  (see p. 10 for
  recipe)
5 lettuce leaves
pepper

1. Clean the spring onions, removing the roots and any withered green parts. Slice them, finely cut the green parts and use them to garnish the soup.
2. Wash the red pepper, remove the seeds and cut into thin strips.
3. Wash the beansprouts and remove the dark roots.
4. Peel the carrot and slice thinly.
5. Heat the oil and sauté the vegetables for a short time only.
6. Add the soy sauce and the stock and bring to the boil.
7. Just before serving, add the lettuce to the soup and garnish with the onion greens. Season with pepper.

Pumpkin Soup

(serves 4)

1 small pumpkin
1 onion
1 tbsp oil
1.5 litres (2½ pints;
  6 cups) vegetable
  stock (see p. 10 for
  recipe)
fresh parsley,
  chopped

1. Peel the pumpkin and cut into pieces, discarding the seeds.
2. Peel and slice the onion.
3. Heat the oil and sauté the pumpkin and onion.
4. Add the stock and cook the soup until the vegetables are ready.
5. Put the soup in a blender and garnish with parsley.

Minestrone
(serves 4)

---

1 carrot
1 celery stalk
¼ cauliflower
1 large potato
¼ celeriac
1 tbsp oil
1.5 litres (2½ pints;
  6 cups) vegetable
  stock (see p. 10 for
  recipe)
1 tsp basil
1 tsp oregano
pepper
Parmesan cheese

1. Peel the carrot and cut into strips.
2. Wash the celery stalk and cut into pieces.
3. Wash the cauliflower and separate into florets.
4. Peel the potato and cut into cubes.
5. Heat the oil and sauté the vegetables for a short time only.
6. Add the stock and cook the soup for 10 minutes.
7. Season with basil, oregano and freshly ground pepper. To add an Italian touch, sprinkle with some grated Parmesan cheese.

Fine Herb Cream Soup
(serves 4)

---

2 tbsp mixed, fresh,
  herbs minced, (e.g.
  tarragon, fennel,
  chervil, chives, basil)
½ onion
½ leek
1 fennel root
1 celery stalk
1 tbsp butter
1.5 litres (2½ pints;
  6 cups) vegetable
  stock (see p. 10 for
  recipe)
cream
basil

1. Peel the onion and chop finely.
2. Clean the leek (removing any roots and green parts), fennel root and celery, and finely chop.
3. Heat the butter in a large saucepan, add the vegetables and sauté for a while.
4. Add the stock and bring the soup to the boil. Add the herbs and blend the soup if required.
5. Just before serving, stir in some cream. Decorate the soup with a few leaves of basil.

Cold Cucumber Soup

(serves 4)

1 cucumber
½ litre (1 pint;
  2 cups) yoghurt
½ lemon
3 fresh mint leaves
½ tbsp chives,
  chopped
1 garlic clove,
  minced
1 parsley sprig,
  chopped

1. Peel the cucumber and shred or purée.
2. Add the yoghurt and the juice of half a lemon.
3. Season with mint, chives, garlic and parsley.

(This is very refreshing in hot weather.)

Artichoke Bisque

(serves 4)

---

3 large globe
  artichokes
1 tbsp lemon juice
2 tbsp olive oil
2 garlic cloves,
  minced
1 litre (1¾ pints;
  4 cups) water
1 small onion
1 tbsp butter
700 ml (1¼ pints;
  3 cups) vegetable
  stock (see p. 10 for
  recipe)
cayenne pepper
fresh basil
125 ml (¼ pint;
  ½ cup) cream

1. Wash the artichokes and cut off the stalks, leaving 1 cm (½ inch). Bend the outermost leaves until they break off and then cut the rest of the leaves off, leaving the lower part. Separate the leaves from the bases.
2. Bring the lemon juice, olive oil, water and garlic to the boil, and cook the artichoke bases in this. The bases are ready when they can be easily pierced with a fork.
3. Set aside 375 ml (¾ pint; 1½ cups) of the cooking water. Gently boil the leaves. After 20 minutes, drain the leaves and use a spoon to remove and separate the edible pulp. Remove the heart from the artichoke bases and cut off the remaining leaves at the edges.
4. Peel the onion, shred and sauté in the butter.
5. Add the artichoke liquid and stock to the onion.
6. Add the pulp and the chopped artichoke bases to the soup. Let the soup heat through for a while and purée.
7. Season with cayenne pepper and basil. Add the cream and serve the soup hot.

Salads

Gardener's Salad

(serves 4)

½ head of lettuce
½ cauliflower
200 g (7 oz) French
  beans
2 tomatoes
½ cucumber
fresh parsley,
  chopped
salad dressing or
  mayonnaise (see
  Dressings and Sauces
  for recipes)

1. Wash and dry the lettuce.
2. Wash and separate the cauliflower into florets.
3. Steam or boil the cauliflower and allow to cool.
4. Clean the French beans. Steam or cook and let them cool.
5. Wash the tomatoes and cut into pieces.
6. Peel the cucumber and slice thinly.
7. Arrange the vegetables on a large dish and sprinkle with the parsley.
8. Serve the salad with a salad dressing or with mayonnaise.

Fine Asparagus Salad

(serves 4)

---

1 bundle green
  asparagus
1 bundle white
  asparagus
mustard sauce (see
  p. 117 for recipe)
mustard and cress

1. Carefully peel the green and white asparagus.
2. Remove the fibrous parts and cut the asparagus into equal pieces. Set aside the asparagus tips. Cook the rest in water. Do not add the asparagus tips until the last 5 minutes.
3. Drain the asparagus on an asparagus dish or on a clean table napkin.
4. Put the asparagus on a dish and coat with mustard sauce. Garnish with mustard and cress.

Corn-Cheese Salad

(serves 4)

---

150 g (5 oz) cooked
sweetcorn or
minicobs
150 g (5 oz) gouda
cheese
6 endive leaves
½ red pepper
8 cherry tomatoes
salad dressing or
mayonnaise (see
Dressings and Sauces
for recipes)

1. Remove the rind from the cheese and cut into cubes and add to the drained corn.
2. Wash the endive leaves and cut into strips.
3. Wash the red pepper, remove the seeds and slice thinly.
4. Wash and cut the tomatoes in half.
5. Add all vegetables to the cheese and corn and toss the salad until well mixed.
6. Serve with a salad dressing or with mayonnaise.

Potato Salad

(serves 4)

---

600 g (1 lb 4 oz)
  potatoes
2 shallots
5 tbsp mayonnaise
  (see p. 114 for
  recipe)
chives
parsley

1. Thoroughly scrub the potatoes and boil them in their skins. Let them cool, peel and slice them.
2. Peel the shallots, chop finely and add to the potato slices.
3. Add the mayonnaise.
4. Wash, pat dry and finely chop the chives and parsley and blend with the potato salad.

(See also recipe on p. 83.)

Avocado with Lamb's Lettuce

(serves 2)

---

300 g (11 oz)
  lamb's lettuce
2 ripe avocados
lemon juice
pepper
basil
12 cherry tomatoes
1 yellow pepper

1. Wash the lettuce, dry and divide among 4 plates.
2. Peel the avocados and remove the stones. Slice 1 avocado and sprinkle with lemon juice to avoid discoloration. Arrange the avocado slices on the 4 plates.
3. Purée the other avocado, add lemon juice, and flavour with pepper and basil.
4. Divide the purée among the plates and garnish with the tomatoes and cubes of yellow pepper.

Stuffed Tomatoes from Warmer Regions

(serves 2)

4 large beefsteak
tomatoes
¼ courgette
¼ yellow pepper
2 tbsp boiled
sweetcorn
5 green pitted olives
1 fresh tarragon
sprig
2 tbsp vinaigrette
(see p. 114 for
recipe)
½ tsp mustard
curly endive

1. Wash the tomatoes, dry, cut off the bottom and carefully scoop out with a teaspoon. Put the tomatoes upside down on a plate, allowing the juice to drain. Set aside the tomato flesh for preparing a soup.
2. Peel and shred the courgette.
3. Wash the pepper, remove the seeds, shred and blend with the courgette.
4. Add the sweetcorn, together with the olives, cut into pieces, and the tarragon.
5. Pour the vinaigrette and mustard onto the salad and refrigerate for an hour.
6. Fill the tomatoes with the salad and garnish them with a few leaves of endive.

Festive Red Chicory Salad

(serves 2)

3 red chicory spears
100 g (4 oz) lamb's
lettuce
100 g (4 oz) curly
endive
6 radishes
2 tbsp walnut oil
½ tbsp ground
mustard seeds
1½ tbsp lemon juice
cayenne pepper
10 shelled walnuts

1. Wash the chicory, remove the bitter core and chop finely.
2. Wash the lettuce and endive, pat dry (finely cut the curly endive) and add to the red chicory.
3. Wash the radishes, remove any green parts, slice and blend with the salad.
4. Blend the walnut oil, mustard seeds and lemon juice and season with cayenne pepper.
5. Garnish with the walnuts.

Red Cabbage Salad
(serves 2)

¼ small red cabbage
1 shallot
1½ tbsp red wine vinegar
1 tsp mustard
4 tbsp olive oil
parsley

1. Wash the red cabbage, dry and slice finely (using bread-slicer or food processor).
2. Peel the shallot, slice and add the vinegar, mustard and olive oil.
3. Pour the dressing onto the red cabbage and garnish with parsley.
4. Refrigerate the red cabbage salad for a few hours (preferably overnight) before serving.

Mixed Salad with Roasted Sesame Seeds
(serves 2)

400 g (14 oz) mixed greens (e.g. crinkly lettuce, endive salad, raddichio, lamb's lettuce)
2 tbsp walnut oil
3 tbsp sesame seeds

1. Wash the mixed greens, dry and tear into small pieces.
2. Put the salad in a large bowl and coat with walnut oil.
3. Lightly roast the sesame seeds in a pan and sprinkle on to the salad.

(You can also use pine nuts, croûtons, sunflower seeds, etc.)

Greek Salad

(serves 2)

150 g (5 oz) lamb's
  lettuce
½ raddichio
4 curly endive leaves
150 g (5 oz) Feta
  cheese
5 black olives
5 green olives
1 green pepper
3 or 4 tbsp
  vinaigrette (see
  p. 114 for recipe)

1. Wash the lettuce, dry and put on to a dish.
2. Wash the raddichio and endive, cut in strips and add to the lettuce.
3. Cut the Feta cheese into cubes and spread over the salad.
4. Garnish with the black and green olives and green pepper.
5. Coat with vinaigrette and serve.

Southern Potato Salad

(serves 2)

---

500 g (1 lb 2 oz)
  potatoes
½ head of lettuce
6 green stuffed olives
2 tbsp olive oil
1 tsp mustard
fresh oregano

1. Scrub the potatoes and boil in their skins. Allow them to cool and then slice them.
2. Wash the lettuce, dry, arrange on a dish and put the potatoes on top.
3. Garnish the salad with green olives, sliced thinly.
4. Prepare a dressing of olive oil, mustard and fresh oregano. Pour this dressing on to the potatoes and serve.

Asparagus–Avocado Salad

(serves 4)

---

500 g (1 lb 2 oz)
  mixed asparagus
  (white and green)
4 lettuce leaves
100 g (5 oz)
  mushrooms
1 avocado
1½ tbsp sherry
  vinegar
3 tbsp oil
1 tbsp mustard seed,
  ground
mustard and cress

1. Carefully peel the asparagus and cut into equal pieces. Cook the asparagus pieces (do not add the tips until the last 5 minutes). Allow the asparagus to cool and then drain. Put the pieces on a dish.
2. Wash the lettuce, pat dry and tear into small pieces.
3. Rub the mushrooms clean and slice thinly. Blend the lettuce with the asparagus and the mushrooms.
4. Peel the avocado, remove the stone, cut into cubes and sprinkle with lemon juice to avoid discoloration.
5. Mix the avocado cubes with the salad and coat with a dressing made from sherry vinegar, oil and ground mustard seed.
6. Garnish the salad with mustard and cress.

Southern Red Chicory Salad

(serves 2)

---

1 yellow pepper
2 spears red chicory pepper
5 green stuffed olives
2 tomatoes
2 tbsp mustard
3 tbsp olive oil
fresh basil
paprika

1. Wash the yellow pepper, remove the seeds and cut into pieces.
2. Wash the red chicory, pat dry, slice thinly and blend with the pepper.
3. Slice the green olives.
4. Wash the tomatoes, slice and mix with the salad together with the olives. Coat with a dressing made from mustard and olive oil.
5. Season with fresh basil, pepper and paprika.

New Orleans Coleslaw

(serves 4)

¼ red cabbage
¼ white cabbage
3 carrots
3 spring onions
½ yellow pepper
60 ml (⅛ pint; ¼ cup) sour cream
60 ml (⅛ pint; ¼ cup) mayonnaise (see p. 114 for recipe)
2 tbsp lemon juice
1 tbsp fresh parsley, chopped
1 tbsp celery leaf, chopped
1 tbsp onion, shredded
cayenne pepper

1. Wash the red and white cabbages, cut into strips (using a bread-slicer or a shredder).
2. Peel and shred the carrots.
3. Wash the spring onions, remove the roots and slice finely.
4. Wash the yellow pepper, remove the seeds and cut into strips. Put the vegetables in a bowl and mix.
5. Blend the sour cream, mayonnaise and lemon juice. Season this dressing with fresh parsley, celery leaf, shredded onion and cayenne pepper. Thoroughly blend the dressing with the vegetables.

Radicchio Salad

(serves 4)

1 radicchio
100 g (4 oz) lamb's
  lettuce
1 avocado
lemon juice
1 tsp mustard
3 tbsp yoghurt
1 tbsp mayonnaise
  (see p. 114 for
  recipe)
pepper
fresh herbs

1. Wash the radicchio and cut finely.
2. Wash the lettuce, pat dry and add to the radicchio.
3. Peel the avocado, remove the stone and cut the flesh into pieces. Sprinkle the avocado with lemon juice (to avoid discoloration) and blend with the salad.
4. Prepare a dressing of mustard, yoghurt and mayonnaise. Season with pepper. Garnish with some chopped herbs.

Creamy Cucumber Salad

(serves 2)

1 cucumber
½ shallot
125 ml (¼ pint;
  ½ cup) cream
1 tbsp mayonnaise
  (see p. 114 for
  recipe)
1 tbsp parsley,
  chopped
1 tbsp dill, chopped
salt

1. Peel the cucumber and slice thinly (in a food processor).
2. Peel the shallot, chop finely and add to the cucumber.
3. Add the cream and mayonnaise. Season with parsley, dill and if necessary, salt.

Tomatoes with Curd Cheese Filling

(serves 2)

4 tomatoes
200 g (7 oz) low-fat
curd cheese
100 g (4 oz)
(unsweetened)
whipped cream
pepper
10 leaves of basil

1. Wash and dry the tomatoes. Cut off the bottom part and scoop out the flesh using a teaspoon. Drain the tomatoes upside down on a plate.
2. Blend low-fat curd cheese with the cream and pepper.
3. Wash the basil, pat dry and chop finely.
4. Blend the basil with the mixture and fill the tomatoes with this mixture. Serve on a bed of lettuce.

White Cabbage Salad

(serves 4)

600 g (1 lb 5 oz)
white cabbage
1 garlic clove,
minced
1 tbsp white wine
vinegar
4 tbsp water
pepper
oregano
salt

1. Wash the white cabbage and cut into strips (using a bread-slicer or food processor). Boil the cabbage strips for 5 minutes and strain.
2. Meanwhile, prepare a dressing of garlic, vinegar, water, pepper, oregano and, if necessary, salt.
3. Pour the dressing on to the hot cabbage strips and allow it to marinate for a few hours.

Celeriac Salad

(serves 4)

---

1 celeriac
1 lemon
2 tbsp mayonnaise
(see p. 114 for recipe)
fresh chives

1. Peel and shred the celeriac. Add the lemon juice to avoid discoloration.
2. Add the mayonnaise and blend with the celeriac.
3. Wash the chives and shred over the salad.

(This salad can also be prepared with carrots or a combination of carrots and celeriac.)

White Cabbage Dressed for Summer

(serves 4)

¼ white cabbage
1 cup vinaigrette
(see p. 114 for recipe)
200 g (7 oz) lamb's lettuce
black olives
½ red pepper
½ green pepper
tomato slices
cucumber

1. Wash the white cabbage, dry, shred and add the vinaigrette. Toss and set aside for a couple of hours.
2. Wash the lettuce, dry and arrange on a dish.
3. Put the cabbage on top of the lettuce and garnish with black olives, peppers, tomato slices and cucumber.

Corn Salad

(serves 4)

---

250 g (9 oz) cooked
  sweetcorn
2 young carrots
1 small courgette
12 cherry tomatoes
1 green pepper
½ red onion
100 g (3 oz) black
  olives
2 tsp capers
6 tbsp olive oil
3 tbsp white wine
  vinegar
1 tsp lime juice
1 tsp mustard
1 tbsp fresh
  tarragon, minced
cayenne pepper

1. Drain the sweetcorn.
2. Peel the carrots and courgette and slice thinly.
3. Wash and cut the tomatoes in half.
4. Wash the green pepper, remove the seeds and cut into strips.
5. Peel the onion and slice into thin rings.
6. Put all the vegetables into a large bowl with the black olives and the capers and mix well.
7. Make the dressing by blending the olive oil, vinegar, lime juice, mustard and fresh tarragon. Season with cayenne pepper.

Southern Salad

(serves 2)

½ cucumber
2 tomatoes
½ onion
½ yellow pepper
½ red pepper
125 ml (¼ pint;
  ½ cup) vinaigrette
  (see p. 114 for
  recipe)
6 black olives

1. Peel and slice the cucumber.
2. Wash the tomatoes, slice and add to the cucumber slices.
3. Peel the onions and cut into rings.
4. Wash the yellow and red peppers, remove the seeds and cut into strips. Mix with the cucumber, tomato and onion.
5. Coat with the vinaigrette and set aside in the refrigerator for an hour.
6. Garnish with black olives.

Leek Salad

(serves 4)

8 leeks
1 garlic clove
1 tsp mustard
125 ml (¼ pint;
½ cup) oil
60 ml (⅛ pint; ¼ cup)
white wine vinegar
1 tbsp fresh lemon
juice
chives, chopped

1. Wash the leeks (removing any roots and green parts) and boil for 15 minutes with the garlic. Drain the leeks and arrange on a dish.
2. Blend the mustard, oil, vinegar and lemon juice and pour on to the leeks.
3. Garnish with chives. Put the leek salad in the refrigerator for 1 or 2 hours, allowing the dressing to soak in.

Spicy Oyster Mushroom Salad
(serves 4)

300 g (11 oz) oyster mushrooms
1 tbsp butter
1 garlic clove
chicken spices (a spicy mixture of herbs for chicken dishes)
cayenne pepper
1 head of lettuce
10 cherry tomatoes
50 g (2 oz) pecan nuts
½ tsp fresh thyme

1. Rub the mushrooms clean and fry in butter with the garlic.
2. Sprinkle the mushrooms with the chicken spices and cayenne pepper. Cook until brown.
3. Wash the lettuce, dry and tear. Put it in a bowl and mix with the mushrooms, tomatoes, pecan nuts and thyme.

Spicy Avocado
(appetizer for 2)

1 ripe avocado
1 green celery stalk
1 tbsp lemon juice
1 tsp curry powder
4 red lettuce leaves
2 slices lemon
2 black olives

1. Cut the avocado in half and remove the stone. Carefully scoop out the flesh and purée with the washed celery. Add lemon juice to prevent discoloration and flavour with curry powder.
2. Wash the lettuce, pat dry and arrange on 2 plates. Fill the avocado halves with the avocado purée.
3. Garnish with lemon slices and black olives.

Mushroom Salad

(side dish for 4)

---

250 g (9 oz)
  mushrooms
lemon juice
½ onion
1 bundle chervil
chives
125 ml (¼ pint;
  ½ cup) vinaigrette
  (see p. 114 for
  recipe)
1 garlic clove,
  minced

1. Rub the mushrooms clean and remove the lower parts of the stalks. Slice the mushrooms and sprinkle with lemon juice.
2. Peel and finely chop the onion.
3. Wash and chop the chervil and a few blades of chives. Mix with the mushrooms and the finely chopped onion.
4. Season with garlic. Pour on to the mushroom salad. Refrigerate for an hour.

Mixed Salad with Tomato Vinaigrette

(serves 2)

½ cucumber
2 tomatoes
½ yellow pepper
3 leaves Chinese
  cabbage or iceberg
  lettuce
tomato vinaigrette
  (see p. 115 for
  recipe)

1. Peel and slice the cucumber.
2. Wash the tomatoes, cut into pieces and add to the cucumber.
3. Wash the yellow pepper, remove the seeds and cut finely.
4. Wash the cabbage or lettuce and cut into strips. Mix the vegetables well and serve with a tomato vinaigrette.

Mexican Stuffed Tomatoes

(serves 2)

4 large tomatoes
¼ green pepper
40 g (2 oz) cooked
sweetcorn
40 g (2 oz) medium
cheese
lamb's lettuce

1. Wash the tomatoes, cut off the tops and scoop out. Set aside the flesh for a soup.
2. Wash the green pepper, remove the seeds and chop finely.
3. Add the sweetcorn.
4. Cut the cheese into cubes and add to the vegetable mixture. Blend well and fill the tomatoes with the mixture.
5. Arrange the tomatoes on a bed of lettuce.

Raw Vegetables with Dips

(serves 2)

---

1 cucumber
10 radishes
10 mushrooms
3 carrots
cherry tomatoes
dips: yoghurt
  dressing, aïoli,
  cocktail sauce,
  Istanbul garlic
  sauce (for recipes
  see *Dressings and
  Sauces*)

1. Peel the cucumber and cut into strips of approximately 8 cm (3 inches) length.
2. Wash the radishes, cutting off any green parts, leaving 3 cm (1 inch) to make them easy to hold.
3. Rub the mushrooms clean, blanch or steam and let them cool.
4. Peel the carrots and cut into strips of approximately 8 cm (3 inches).
5. Wash the tomatoes, pat dry and put a cocktail stick in each one.
6. Arrange the vegetables on one large dish. Serve with a few dips.

Fennel Salad

(serves 2)

---

2 fennel roots
½ red lettuce
125 ml (¼ pint;
  ½ cup) olive oil
60 ml (⅛ pint; ¼ cup)
  wine vinegar
fennel green
basil
oregano
paprika
green stuffed olives

1. Wash the fennel roots. Remove any green parts and save for garnishing. Roughly shred or finely cut the roots.
2. Wash the lettuce, cut into strips and add to the fennel.
3. To make the dressing blend the oil and the vinegar and season with basil, oregano and paprika.
4. Garnish with the green parts from the fennel and green stuffed olives.

Spicy Tomato Salad

(serves 2)

---

4 tomatoes
2 garlic cloves
1 onion
6 black olives
1 tbsp olive oil
fresh basil
dried oregano
salt
pepper

1. Wash the tomatoes, slice and arrange on a large dish.
2. Peel the garlic, slice and divide among the tomatoes.
3. Peel the onion, cut into rings and add to the salad.
4. Garnish with black olives.
5. Pour the olive oil on to the salad and sprinkle with some finely chopped fresh basil and dried oregano. Season with salt and pepper, if necessary.

Sour Stuffed Tomatoes

(serves 2)

---

4 tomatoes
4 tbsp pickled
  vegetables
1 pickled gherkin
1 pickled onion
lettuce

1. Wash the tomatoes, cut off the tops, scoop out the flesh (keep this to make soup) and drain upside down.
2. Mix the pickled vegetables with the pickled gherkin (cut finely) and pickled onions.
3. Fill the tomatoes with this mixture and arrange them on a plate with the lettuce.

Refreshing Olives

(snack for 4 to 5)

20 green pitted olives
1 carrot
½ yellow pepper
1 winter radish

1. Cut the carrot, yellow pepper and radish into tiny pieces.
2. Insert a piece of each vegetable into each olive.
3. Serve any remaining vegetable pieces with the olives.

Green Potato Salad

(serves 4)

1 kg (2 lb 4 oz) new potatoes
1 shallot
1 bundle dill
1 bundle parsley
5 sage leaves
1 lemon balm sprig
2 tbsp mayonnaise (see p. 114 for recipe)
1 tbsp sour cream

1. Scrub the potatoes, boil in their skins until cooked. Peel and slice.
2. Peel the shallot and chop.
3. Wash the dill, parsley, sage and lemon balm, pat dry and chop finely or cut.
4. Blend the mayonnaise with the sour cream and mix with the fresh herbs. Blend this sauce with the potato slices.

Raw Vegetable Salad

(serves 1)

¼ Chinese cabbage
¼ cucumber
¼ red pepper
1 tomato
2 tbsp cooked sweetcorn
2 tbsp yoghurt dressing or vinaigrette (see pp. 114–15 for recipes)

1. Wash the Chinese cabbage leaves, pat dry, cut into strips.
2. Peel and slice the cucumber.
3. Cut the red pepper into strips.
4. Cut the tomato into pieces.
5. Mix the cucumber, red pepper and tomato together with the sweetcorn.
6. Add the yoghurt dressing or vinaigrette.

Radish Salad

(serves 4)

---

1 bundle radishes
½ cucumber
6 lettuce leaves
3 tbsp horseradish,
  creamed

1. Remove the stalks from the radishes, wash and slice.
2. Wash the cucumber and slice.
3. Wash the lettuce, pat dry, cut finely and add to the radishes and cucumber.
4. Add the creamed horseradish and blend well.
5. Serve with a green salad or with bread.

Fruit Preparations

Tropical Mango Cocktail
(serves 4)

1 ripe mango
6 lychees
1 ripe banana
3 passion fruit
125 ml (¼ pint;
½ cup) of double
cream

1. Peel the mango, remove the stone and cut into pieces.
2. Peel the lychees, remove the stones and add to the mango pieces.
3. Peel the banana, slice thinly, sprinkle with lemon juice to prevent discoloration and add to the rest.
4. Cut the passion fruit in half. Use a teaspoon to scoop out the flesh and blend with the fruit salad.
5. Beat the cream and serve with the mango cocktail.

Stuffed Pineapple
(serves 2)

1 fresh pineapple
2 ripe pears
2 oranges
1 kiwi fruit
125 ml (¼ pint;
½ cup) double
cream

1. Cut the pineapple in half (set aside 1 half). Remove the hard core and scoop out using a grapefruit knife. Cut the flesh into bite-sized pieces, peel and put in a bowl.
2. Peel the pears, remove the cores, cut into pieces and add to the pineapple pieces.
3. Peel the oranges until the flesh becomes visible and use a sharp knife to separate the segments.
4. Mix the fruit pieces and fill the hollow part of the pineapple.
5. Serve with cream.

6. Peel the kiwi fruit, slice thinly and garnish the pineapple with it.
7. Beat the cream and serve with the pineapple.

Winter Pineapple

(serves 2)

---

1 pineapple
2 apples
2 mandarin oranges
100 g (4 oz; ½ cup) hazelnuts

1. Cut the pineapple in half lengthwise (set aside 1 half). Remove the hard core, scoop out, cut the flesh into pieces, peel and put in a bowl.
2. Peel the apples, remove the cores, cut into pieces and mix with the pineapple pieces.

3. Peel the oranges, separate the segments and put into a bowl. Roughly chop.
4. Mix the fruit salad well and fill the pineapple half with it. Sprinkle with chopped hazelnuts and serve.

Cinnamon Apples
(serves 2)

---

4 apples
½ lemon
1 apple
2 tbsp hazelnuts,
  ground
½ tsp cinnamon

1. Wash the 4 apples, dry and remove the cores using an apple corer, creating a hollow. Steam them.
2. Squeeze the lemon and rub the juice into the apple hollows to prevent discoloration.
3. Roughly shred the single apple, sprinkle with a few drops of lemon juice and blend with the hazelnuts and cinnamon.
4. Fill the apple hollows with the apple and cinnamon mixture and serve.

Stuffed Pear on a Bed of Strawberries
(serves 2)

---

2 large, ripe pears
lemon juice
10 strawberries
4 passion fruit

1. Peel the pears and cut in half. Remove the cores and sprinkle the pears with lemon juice to prevent discoloration.
2. Wash the strawberries (if unavailable use 2 kiwi fruit), remove the stalks and slice thinly. Arrange the slices overlapping on 4 plates.
3. Cut the passion fruit in half, scoop out the flesh and fill the pear halves with it. Arrange the pears on a bed of strawberries and serve.

Citrus Salad
(serves 2)

2 oranges
1 pink grapefruit
2 mandarin oranges
1 bunch black
 grapes
2 tbsp almond flakes

1. Peel the oranges, separate into segments as described under 'Stuffed pineapple' on p. 46 and put the segments in a bowl.
2. Peel the grapefruit and separate into segments. Put the segments into the same bowl as the oranges. Peel the mandarin oranges and separate into segments. Add to the bowl.
3. Wash the grapes, remove them from their stems, cut in half and remove the seeds (also remove the skin if necessary). Mix the fruit well, divide the salad between 2 bowls and sprinkle with the almond flakes.

Fruit Salad
(serves 4)

1 pear
1 orange
1 bunch grapes
½ pineapple
2 tbsp raisins soaked
 in 2 tbsp water
whipped cream

1. Peel the pear, remove the core and cut the flesh into pieces.
2. Thickly peel the orange and separate into segments (as described under 'Stuffed pineapple' on p. 46).
3. Wash the grapes, remove them from their stems, cut in half and remove the seeds.
4. Peel the pineapple, remove the hard core and cut into pieces.
5. Add the soaked raisins and their liquid.
6. Mix all the ingredients and serve with whipped cream.

Honeydew Melon Cocktail

(serves 2)

---

1 honeydew melon
1 apple
1 tbsp lemon juice
1 banana
1 mandarin orange
2 tbsp cashew nuts,
   chopped

1. Cut the melon in half, remove the seeds, creating a hollow.
2. Peel the apple, remove the core, cut in to pieces and sprinkle with lemon juice to prevent discoloration.
3. Also add the banana, cut into slices.
4. Peel the mandarin orange, separate into segments and add to the fruit salad.
5. Mix well and fill the hollow of the melon with the cocktail. Garnish with cashew nuts.

Refreshing Sour Summer Salad

(serves 4)

---

2 peaches
2 plums
4 apricots
2 nectarines
sour cream

1. Wash the peaches, cut in half, remove the stones and cut into pieces.
2. Repeat with plums, apricots and nectarines.
3. Mix the fruit well and serve with sour cream.

Layers of Fruit Salad

(serves 4)

---

1 pomegranate
2 oranges
1 avocado
lemon juice
½ pineapple
2 kiwi fruit
200 g (7 oz) strawberries
1 mango
125 ml (¼ pint; ½ cup) orange juice, freshly squeezed
lemon balm

1. Use a tall glass container or a square vase. Cut the pomegranate in half and remove the seeds.
2. Peel the oranges and separate into segments.
3. Peel the avocado, slice and sprinkle with lemon juice to avoid discoloration.
4. Peel the pineapple, remove the hard core and cut the flesh into pieces.
5. Peel the kiwi fruit and slice.
6. Wash the strawberries, remove the stalks and slice.
7. Peel the mango, remove the stone and slice.
8. Arrange the fruit in layers, starting with a layer of pomegranate, followed by a layer of orange, avocado, pineapple, kiwi fruit, strawberry and mango.
9. Coat the fruit salad with the orange juice and garnish with lemon balm.

Forest-Fruit Cocktail

(serves 2)

---

100 g (4 oz)
  blueberries
100 g (4 oz)
  raspberries
100 g (4 oz)
  blackberries
100 g (4 oz) currants
4 tbsp (150 g) quark

1. Wash the fruit, pat dry.
2. Divide the cocktail among 4 bowls and coat with quark.

Sweet Avocado Salad

(serves 2)

---

1 ripe avocado
1 mango
1 orange
1 kiwi fruit
1 apple
yoghurt dressing (see
  p. 115 for recipe)

1. Peel the avocado, remove the stone and cut into pieces.
2. Repeat with the mango.
3. Peel the orange and separate into segments as described under 'Stuffed pineapple' on p. 46.
4. Peel the kiwi fruit and slice.
5. Peel the apple, remove the core and cut into pieces.
6. Mix the fruit well and serve with a yoghurt dressing.

Stuffed Apricots

(serves 2)

8 fresh apricots
2 dried, soaked
  apricots
150 g (5 oz) sour
  cream
8 mint leaves

1. Wash the fresh apricots, cut in half and remove the stones.
2. Drain and chop finely the 2 dried, soaked apricots.
3. Blend the sour cream with the dried apricot pieces.
4. Fill 4 of the apricot halves with the sour cream and use the other 4 halves as a lid.
5. Garnish with mint leaves.

Fried Banana with Ginger

(serves 4)

4 bananas
2 tbsp safflower oil
1 tsp ginger
20 g (1 oz)
  strawberries
1 kiwi fruit

1. Peel the bananas.
2. Heat the oil in a pan. Fry the bananas and flavour with ginger.
3. Wash the strawberries, remove the stalks and slice.
4. Arrange the strawberry slices on 4 plates and put the fried bananas on top.
5. Garnish with slices of kiwi fruit.

Ugli-Grapefruit Salad with Thyme Honey
(serves 4)

---

1 ugli fruit
1 grapefruit
1 orange
1 mandarin orange
5 kumquats
1 tbsp thyme honey
125 ml (¼ pint;
   ½ cup) orange
   juice, freshly
   squeezed
2 tbsp lemon juice
1 tsp thyme

1. Peel the ugli fruit, grapefruit, orange and mandarin orange and separate into segments. Cut the segments into pieces and put in a bowl.
2. Wash the kumquats, slice and add to the citrus fruit.
3. Heat the honey, orange and lemon juices and flavour with thyme. Pour the honey sauce over the citrus salad, let it cool, mix and serve.

Sharon Fruit Salad
(serves 2)

---

2 sharon fruit
1 banana
2 kiwi fruit
4 passion fruit
whipped cream

1. Wash the sharon fruit, dry and cut into pieces.
2. Peel the banana, slice and sprinkle with lemon juice to prevent discoloration.
3. Peel and slice the kiwi fruit.
4. Put all the fruit in a bowl and mix.
5. Cut the passion fruit in half and blend the flesh with the salad.
6. Serve with whipped cream.

Pineapple Salad with Coconut
(serves 4)

½ pineapple
200 g (7 oz)
  raspberries
100 g (3.5 oz;
  ½ cup) raisins
soaked in 2 tbsp
water
1 banana
3 tbsp flaked coconut

1. Peel the pineapple, remove the hard core and cut into pieces.
2. Wash the raspberries, remove the stalks and add to the pineapple pieces.
3. Soak the raisins (the night before). Pour the raisins and their liquid over the salad.
4. Peel the banana, slice and combine with the salad.
5. Sprinkle the coconut over the pineapple salad and serve.

Summer Fruits in Forest-Fruit Sauce
(serves 4)

400 g (14 oz) forest-
  fruits (e.g.
  blueberries,
  blackberries,
  raspberries,
  strawberries)
2 peaches
2 apricots
4 fresh pineapple
  slices
2 tbsp blueberries
4 mint leaves
whipped cream

1. Wash the forest-fruits, remove the stalks and purée. Strain the fruit purée. Pour on to 4 dessert plates.
2. Wash the peaches, dry, cut into 4 pieces and slice.
3. Wash the apricots, dry and divide into 4.
4. Arrange the peaches, apricots and pineapple on the forest-fruit sauce.
5. Garnish with blueberries, mint and whipped cream.

Avocado Mousse

(serves 4)

---

2 ripe avocados
1 grapefruit
3 tbsp whipped
  cream
lemon balm leaves

1. Cut the avocados in half, remove the stones and scoop out the flesh with a small spoon.
2. Purée the avocado flesh with the juice of half of the grapefruit until smooth and creamy.
3. Blend with the whipped cream and fill the avocado halves with it. Garnish with grapefruit slices from the remaining half and lemon balm leaves.

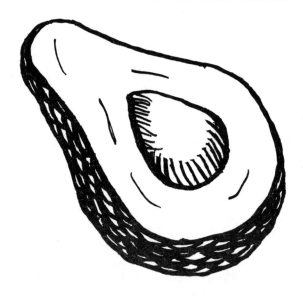

Fig Cocktail

(serves 2)

5 fresh figs
2 peaches
1 banana
lemon juice
125 ml (¼ pint;
  ½ cup) whipped
  cream
1 tbsp lemon juice
1 tbsp washed
  grated lemon peel
fresh lemon balm

1. Wash the figs and cut into 4 pieces.
2. Wash the peaches, cut in half, remove the stones and slice.
3. Peel the banana, slice and sprinkle with lemon juice to avoid discoloration. Mix the fruit well.
4. Blend the whipped cream with the lemon juice and peel. Divide the fig cocktail between 2 plates. Put the lemon cream on top.
5. Garnish with lemon balm.

Melon Cocktail with Mint

(serves 4)

3 tbsp mint leaves,
  chopped
125 ml (¼ pint;
  ½ cup) water
1 tbsp honey
1 lemon
1 orange
1 honeydew melon
6 whole mint leaves

1. Put the chopped mint leaves in a small bowl.
2. Blend the water and honey and let this mixture boil gently for 5 minutes. Pour it over the chopped mint leaves, let it cool and then strain.
3. Add the juice of the lemon and orange.
4. Scoop out the melon using a melon scoop.
5. Fill 6 cocktail glasses with the melon and coat with the mint syrup.
6. Garnish with mint leaves.

Banana–Lemon Balm Purée with Strawberries

(serves 4)

2 bananas
½ lemon
8 lemon balm leaves
125 g (5 oz)
  strawberries
whipped cream

1. Peel the bananas and purée. Add the juice of half a lemon.
2. Wash the lemon balm, pat dry, chop half the leaves finely and blend with the banana purée.
3. Wash the strawberries, pat dry, remove the stalks and slice.
4. Arrange the strawberries and the banana purée on 4 dessert plates.
5. Garnish with whipped cream and the rest of the lemon balm leaves.

Apple Sauce with Spicy Raspberry Topping

(serves 4)

6 apples
½ lemon
100 g (4 oz)
  raspberries
¼ tsp ginger
¼ tsp vanilla powder
¼ tsp nutmeg
4 mint leaves

1. Peel the apples, remove the cores and shred finely. Add the juice of half a lemon to prevent discoloration.
2. Wash the raspberries, remove the stalks (except for the stalks of the 4 raspberries that will serve as decoration) and purée.
3. Flavour the topping with ginger, vanilla and nutmeg.
4. Divide the apple among 4 small bowls and pour some topping on it.
5. Garnish with the 4 raspberries and mint leaves.

Blanched Pears with Marjoram

(serves 4)

4 pears
125 ml (¼ pint;
  ½ cup) grape or
  apple juice
2 tbsp lemon juice
2 marjoram sprigs

1. Peel the pears, cut in half, remove the cores.
2. Heat the grape or apple juice, lemon juice and marjoram and blanch the pears in it.
3. Serve hot or cold.

Apple Cocktail

(serves 4)

---

2 apples
125 ml (¼ pint;
  ½ cup) fresh orange
  juice
6 apricots
½ tsp ginger
whipped cream
½ tsp cinnamon

1. Peel the apples, remove the cores and cut into strips.
2. Coat the apples with orange juice.
3. Wash the apricots, cut into 4 pieces, remove the stones and add to the apple pieces.
4. Flavour this cocktail with ginger.
5. Serve the salad in 4 cocktail glasses and garnish with whipped cream and cinnamon.

Stone Fruit Salad with Cinnamon

(serves 4)

---

2 peaches
6 apricots
4 plums
2 nectarines
1 orange
½ tsp cinnamon

1. Wash the fruit.
2. Cut all the fruit into 4 pieces, remove the stones and put in a bowl.

3. Pour the juice of the orange on to the fruit, add the cinnamon and mix the salad well.

Warm Dishes

Steamed Vegetables

(serves 4)

---

1 broccoli
½ small cauliflower
4 carrots
1 tbsp butter
1 tbsp flour
180 ml (⅓ pint;
  ¾ cup) vegetable
  stock (see p. 10 for
  recipe)
60 ml (⅛ pint;
  ¼ cup) cream
nu
pe
pr

1. Wash the broccoli, peel the stems and cut into pieces. Separate the rest into florets.
2. Separate the cauliflower into florets and wash thoroughly.
3. Peel and slice the carrots or cut into strips.
4. Steam the vegetables.
5. To prepare the sauce, heat the butter until melted, add the flour, stirring constantly. When the flour has been absorbed by the butter, add the stock while stirring and simmer until the sauce has thickened. Then add the cream.
6. Season the sauce with nutmeg, pepper and paprika.
7. Serve the warm vegetables with the sauce and boiled potatoes.

Chinese Cabbage au Gratin

(serves 4)

---

1 Chinese cabbage
½ tsp stock granules
  or bouillon powder
200 g (7 oz)
  mushrooms
1 tbsp butter
grated gruyère or
  emmental cheese

1. Cut the Chinese cabbage into 4 pieces, wash thoroughly, boil in ample water with stock granules for about 8 minutes and drain. Put the Chinese cabbage pieces in a greased oven dish.
2. Rub the mushrooms clean, slice and stew in butter.

3. Spread the mushrooms over the Chinese cabbage and sprinkle liberally with the cheese.
4. Grill the cabbage dish and serve with a salad.

Stuffed Pepper

(serves 4)

6 large red or yellow peppers
300 g (11 oz) rice
1 onion
1 small green pepper
150 g (5.3 oz) mushrooms
1 tbsp oil
paprika
curry powder
pepper
lettuce

1. Wash the red or yellow peppers, cut the top part off, briefly blanch or steam and drain.
2. Boil the rice.
3. Meanwhile, peel and finely chop the onion.
4. Wash the green pepper, remove the seeds and cut finely.
5. Rub the mushrooms clean and slice.
6. Heat the oil and sauté the onion, add the green pepper, the mushrooms and the boiled rice and season with paprika, curry powder and pepper.
7. Fill the red or yellow peppers with the rice mixture and put on a heat-resistant oven dish with a lid. Let the peppers heat up in a hot oven for 15 minutes.
8. Serve with the fresh lettuce.

Ratatouille

(serves 4)

---

1 courgette
250 g (9 oz)
  mushrooms
1 red pepper
1 large onion
2 garlic cloves
5 or 6 beefsteak
  tomatoes
1 tbsp olive oil
2 bay leaves
½ tbsp stock granules
  or bouillon powder

1. Wash the courgette and slice or cut into pieces.
2. Rub the mushrooms clean, remove the lower part of the stalks and cut in half.
3. Wash the red pepper, remove the seeds and cut into pieces.
4. Peel the onion and cut into rings.
5. Peel the garlic cloves and cut in half.
6. Peel the tomatoes and cut into pieces.
7. Heat the olive oil and sauté the onion rings, adding the rest of the vegetables and mushrooms.
8. Add bay leaves and stock granules. Simmer the vegetables on a low heat until ready.

Steamed Cauliflower with Herb Sauce

(serves 4)

---

1 large cauliflower
1 tbsp butter
1 tbsp flour
250 ml (½ pint;
  1 cup) vegetable
  stock (see p. 10 for
  recipe)
4 tbsp (unsweetened)
  whipped cream
nutmeg
pepper
1 tbsp fresh parsley,
  chopped
2 basil leaves, finely
  shredded

1. Thoroughly wash the cauliflower and steam (separate into florets if preferred).
2. Melt the butter and blend with the flour. When the butter has absorbed the flour completely, add the stock, stirring constantly. Remove the sauce from the heat and blend with the cream. Season with nutmeg, pepper, parsley and basil.
3. Serve with boiled or steamed potatoes.

Mixed Vegetables from the Wok

(serves 4)

1 onion
1 garlic clove
1 red pepper
½ Chinese cabbage
200 g (7 oz)
  mushrooms
200 g (7 oz) broccoli
2 tbsp oil
2 tbsp soy sauce
1 tsp ginger
½ tsp paprika
pepper

1. Peel the onion, cut in half and slice.
2. Peel the garlic and cut into 4 pieces.
3. Wash the pepper, remove the seeds and cut into strips. Wash the Chinese cabbage, pat dry and cut into strips.
4. Rub the mushrooms clean and cut in half.
5. Wash the broccoli, separate into florets and cut the stem into pieces.
6. Heat the oil in a wok and fry the onion for 1 minute while stirring. Add the clove of garlic and the pepper strips and fry for 2 minutes while stirring. Add the broccoli and fry for 1 minute while stirring. Fry the Chinese cabbage and the mushrooms for 1 minute. Season the vegetables with soy sauce, ginger, paprika and pepper.
7. Serve with rice.

Vegetable Strips with Coriander Sauce
(serves 4)

---

100 g (4 oz) carrots
100 g (4 oz) kohlrabi
100 g (4 oz)
  courgettes
1 spring onion
1 tbsp butter
2 tsp ground
  coriander
250 ml (½ pint;
  1 cup) cream

1. Wash the carrots, kohlrabi and cour-gettes and use a peeler to cut them into thin strips like tagliatelle. Only use the outermost part of the courgettes, not the seeds.
2. Blanch or steam the vegetable strips for 2 or 3 minutes.
3. Shred the spring onion and fry in the butter.
4. Add the coriander (or another herb) and cream and pour the sauce over the vegetable strips.

Creamy Brussels Sprouts with Carrot
(serves 4)

---

800 g (1 lb 14 oz)
  Brussels sprouts
6 new carrots
125 ml (¼ pint;
  ½ cup) cream
4 fresh basil leaves,
  chopped
pepper
paprika

1. Clean the sprouts.
2. Wash or peel the carrots and cut into equal-sized pieces. Steam the carrots and sprouts until ready.
3. Heat the cream and add the chopped basil leaves.
4. Flavour with pepper and paprika and serve with pasta or potatoes.

Steamed Carrots with Courgette and Sage

(serves 4)

1 bundle of new carrots
1 courgette
a few sage leaves
1 small onion
1 tbsp butter
125 ml (¼ pint; ½ cup) cream

1. Remove the green parts from the carrots and discard. Wash the carrots.
2. Wash the courgette and cut into slices or cubes. Steam the carrots and courgette.
3. Wash the sage, pat dry and chop finely.
4. Peel the onion and cut finely. Heat the butter and sauté the onion. Add the sage and cream. Pour the dressing on to the steamed hot vegetables and serve with potatoes.

Stuffed Cabbage Rolls with Spicy Rice

(serves 4)

100 g (4 oz) rice
1 small onion
½ red pepper
1 tbsp butter
1 tsp curry powder
1 savoy cabbage

1. Boil the rice and let it cool.
2. Peel and shred the onion.
3. Wash the pepper and cut finely.
4. Heat the butter and sauté the onion and the pepper. Add the rice and curry powder. Fry the rice for a while and remove from the heat.
5. Remove the outermost leaves from the cabbage, wash them and boil in water for 6 minutes. Drain them.
6. Put a spoonful of rice in the middle of each leaf and roll the leaves.
7. Serve the rolls with the rest of the rice and curry mixture.

Broccoli with Leek Cream Sauce

(serves 4)

500 g (18 oz)
  broccoli
1 leek
1 tbsp butter
125 ml (¼ pint;
  ½ cup) cream
  sauce (see p. 121
  for recipe)
curry powder
pepper

1. Wash the broccoli and steam until ready.
2. Remove any green parts from the leek, discard and cut the rest into rings.
3. Heat the butter and stew the leek.
4. Prepare the cream sauce and add the leek to it. Season with curry powder and pepper.
5. Serve the broccoli with the leek cream sauce and potatoes or pasta.

Brussels Sprouts and Cherry Tomatoes in Herb Butter

(serves 2)

300 g (11 oz)
  Brussels sprouts
200 g (7 oz) cherry
  tomatoes
1 or 2 tbsp butter
  with freshly
  chopped herbs

1. Clean the sprouts, wash and cook.
2. Wash and dry the tomatoes.
3. Heat the herb butter and sauté the sprouts and the tomatoes.
4. Serve with a green salad.

Stuffed Mushrooms with Leek
(serves 2)

12 large wild
  mushrooms
1 leek
3 chives
1 tbsp butter
60 ml (⅛ pint; ¼ cup)
  (unsweetened)
  whipped cream
cayenne pepper
paprika

1. Rub the mushrooms clean and finely chop the stalks. (Reserve the mushroom caps for later in the recipe.)
2. Clean and wash the leek, discarding any green parts.
3. Wash the chives, pat dry and shred.
4. Heat the butter and stew the leek and the mushroom stalks. Add the chives and cream.
5. Mix together with cayenne pepper and paprika.
6. Fill the mushrooms with the leek mixture and grill until brown.
7. Serve with pasta.

Aubergine with Tomatoes from the Oven
(serves 4)

3 aubergines
8 beefsteak tomatoes
1 or 2 tbsp olive oil
oregano
basil
Southern salad (see
  p. 35 for recipe)

1. Wash the aubergines, slice, sprinkle with salt and strain for 1 hour.
2. Wash the tomatoes and cut into rings.
3. Sauté the aubergines in the olive oil.
4. Arrange the aubergine slices and the tomatoes alternately in an oven dish.
5. Sprinkle with some oregano and basil and heat the dish in a 200° C (400° F, Gas Mark 6) oven for 40 minutes.
6. Serve with a Southern salad.

Three Vegetables in Cheese Sauce
(serves 4)

---

1 small cauliflower
300 g (11 oz)
  broccoli
4 carrots
cheese sauce (see
  p. 121 for recipe)
parsley, chopped

1. Wash the cauliflower and broccoli and separate into florets.
2. Peel the carrots, cut into equal pieces and steam or boil together with the other vegetables.
3. Prepare the cheese sauce and pour it over the vegetables.
4. Sprinkle some parsley over the vegetables.
5. Serve with a green salad.

Creamy Cucumber

(serves 4)

---

1 shallot
1 cucumber
1 tbsp butter
2 tsp stock granules
  or bouillon powder
125 ml (¼ pint;
  ½ cup) cream
cayenne pepper
2 tbsp fresh dill,
  chopped

1. Peel the shallot and chop finely.
2. Peel the cucumber and cut into equal cubes.
3. Heat the butter and stew the cucumber cubes and shallot.
4. Add the stock granules, stir in the cream. Remove from heat and season with cayenne pepper and dill.
5. Serve with pasta.

Kohlrabi au Gratin

(serves 4)

---

4 kohlrabi
1 small onion
200 g (7 oz)
  mushrooms
1 tbsp butter
1 garlic clove,
  minced
pepper
1 tsp stock granules
  or bouillon powder
100 g (4 oz) low-fat
  grated cheese or
  quark
125 ml (¼ pint;
  ½ cup) cream

1. Peel the kohlrabi and cut into cubes.
2. Peel the onion and chop finely.
3. Rub the mushrooms clean and slice thinly.
4. Heat the butter and stew the onion, kohlrabi and mushrooms.
5. Add the garlic and season with pepper and stock granules.
6. Combine the cheese and cream with the vegetables.
7. Serve hot with a mixed salad.

Stuffed Aubergine

(serves 4)

---

4 small aubergines
1 shallot
½ red pepper
2 tomatoes
1 tbsp olive oil
1 garlic clove,
  minced
2 basil leaves,
  chopped
3 mozzarella
  cheeses

1. Wash the aubergines, cut in half and scoop out the flesh. Cut the flesh into pieces.
2. Peel the shallot and chop finely.
3. Wash the pepper, remove the seeds and cut finely.
4. Skin the tomatoes and cut into pieces.
5. Heat the olive oil and stew the shallot, the aubergine flesh, the pepper and the tomato. Add the garlic.
6. Remove from heat and add the basil.
7. Fill the aubergine halves with the vegetable mixture and put in to a greased oven dish. Slice the mozzarella cheese (using an egg slicer) and spread over the aubergines. Put the dish in a 180° C (350° F, Gas Mark 4) oven for 40 minutes until ready.

Steamed Vegetable Dish
(serves 2)

---

2 fennel roots
½ red pepper
½ yellow pepper
1 onion
3 carrots
1 bay leaf
1 tbsp stock
  granules or bouillon
  powder
2 or 3 tbsp butter
  with freshly
  chopped herbs

1. Cut the fennel into 4 pieces and wash.
2. Wash the peppers, remove the seeds and cut into large pieces.
3. Peel the onion and carrots and slice or cut into large pieces.
4. Put the vegetables into a steaming basket. Add the bay leaf to the water. Steam the vegetables.
5. Put the vegetables on to a dish and spread with herb butter.
6. Serve with potatoes.

Asparagus
(serves 2 to 3)

---

2 bundles asparagus
  (green and/or
  white)
2 parsley sprigs
2 tbsp butter
125 ml (¼ pint;
  ½ cup)
  (unsweetened)
  whipped cream
cayenne pepper

1. Peel the asparagus and steam.
2. Wash the parsley, pat dry and chop finely.
3. Heat the butter until melted, stir in the cream and season with cayenne pepper.
4. Serve with potato puffs (see recipe on p. 79) or new potatoes.

Endive in Pastries

(serves 4)

1 large head of
  endive
butter
125 ml (¼ pint;
  ½ cup) cream
  sauce (for recipe
  see p. 121)
1 garlic clove, minced
stock granules or
  bouillon powder
nutmeg
4 puff pastry cases

1. Wash the endive and boil down adding a little butter.
2. Remove from heat and add the cream sauce.

3. Season with garlic, stock granules and nutmeg. Fill puff pastry cases with the endive mixture and heat them up in a hot oven.

Fried Vegetables

(serves 4)

---

1 shallot
½ red pepper
200 g (7 oz)
  broccoli
100 g (4 oz)
  mushrooms
2 tbsp butter
pepper
paprika
curry powder

1. Peel the shallot and cut finely.
2. Wash the pepper, remove the seeds and cut finely.
3. Wash the broccoli, drain and cut into pieces.
4. Rub the mushrooms clean and slice.
5. Heat the butter and sauté the vegetables. Season with pepper, curry powder and paprika.
6. Serve with mashed potato or rice.

Potato Dishes

Boiled Potatoes
(serves 4)

---

1 kg (2 lb 4 oz)
   potatoes
vegetable stock (see
   p. 10 for recipe) or
   salt
2 bay leaves

1. Peel the potatoes, remove the eyes and cut in half any large ones.
2. Boil the potatoes (for about 15 minutes) in water, to which you have added some stock or salt and bay leaves.
3. For mushy potatoes, shake the cooking pot after pouring off the water.

Potatoes in Skins
(serves 4)

---

1 kg (2 lb 4 oz)
   potatoes
2 bay leaves

1. Wash the potatoes, scrub and boil in their skins with the bay leaves.
2. Pour off the water and serve with or without their skins.

Mashed Potato
(serves 4)

---

1 kg (2 lb 4 oz)
   potatoes
⅛ litre (¼ pint; ½ cup)
   cream
⅛ litre (¼ pint; ½ cup)
   vegetable stock (see
   p. 10 for recipe)
25 g (1 oz) butter
nutmeg
mace
pepper

1. Peel the potatoes, boil them and then pour off the water.
2. Add the cream, stock and butter and purée using a masher or blender. Season with nutmeg, mace and pepper.

Potato Puffs

For potato puffs, make sure the mashed potato is slightly thicker and use a piping bag to squirt the puffs on to a baking tray. Grill until golden brown.

Steamed Potatoes

Peel potatoes, cut in half, put in the steaming basket and steam.

Baked Potatoes

Wash potatoes of equal size, dry and pierce with a fork. Bake the potatoes in a medium hot oven for ¾–1 hour at 200° C (400° F, Gas Mark 6).

Potato au Gratin
(serves 2)

500 g (18 oz) potatoes
1 garlic clove
125 ml (¼ pint; ½ cup) cream
pepper
100 g (3.5 oz; ½ cup) breadcrumbs

1. Peel the potatoes and slice thinly (using a food processor). Steam the potato slices but not for too long or else they will fall apart.
2. Grease a shallow oven dish and rub with garlic. Arrange the potato slices on the dish and coat with cream. Sprinkle with pepper and breadcrumbs.
3. Grill the potatoes until they develop a brown crust.

Oven Chips/French Fries

(serves 4)

---

6 large, firm potatoes
paprika
salt
pepper
4 tbsp oil

1. Peel the potatoes, cut into chips/french fries and spread out on a greased baking tray. Sprinkle with paprika and, if required, salt and pepper.
2. Pour the oil on to the chips/french fries, cover with aluminium foil and bake in a preheated oven at 220° C (425° F, Gas Mark 7) for 30 minutes. Remove the foil and bake the chips/french fries for another 15 minutes or until golden brown. Every now and then, turn them over.

Potato Skins with Sour Cream

(serves 2)

---

4 large, new
  potatoes
butter
herbs
sour cream
chives

1. Scrub the potatoes, boil and then pour off the water. Cut the potatoes lengthwise into 4 pieces. Cut out the flesh with a sharp knife, but leave ½ cm of flesh in the skin.
2. Arrange the potato skins on a greased baking tray and coat with the melted butter. Sprinkle with herbs and bake for 15–20 minutes in a 230° C (450° F, Gas Mark 8) oven until crisp.
3. Serve the potato skins lukewarm or warm with sour cream and chives and a salad.

Stewed Potatoes

(serves 4)

---

1 kg (2 lb 4 oz)
  potatoes
1 onion
1 tbsp butter
1 bay leaf
pepper
stock granules or
  bouillon powder

1. Peel the potatoes and cut into cubes.
2. Peel the onion and cut finely.
3. Heat the butter and stew the potatoes and the onions on a low heat. Add the bay leaf and season with pepper and stock granules.

Fried (New) Potatoes

(serves 4)

---

500 g (18 oz) large
  new potatoes

1. Peel the potatoes and cut out little balls (using a melon scoop).
2. Boil the balls until they are half cooked, pour off the water, pat dry and deep fry until golden brown.

Hotchpotch

(serves 4)

---

mashed potato (see
  recipe on p. 78)
selection of
  vegetables

1. Blend the mashed potato (made from 1 kg of potatoes) with boiled, steamed or raw vegetables (e.g. carrots, cauliflower, spinach).
2. Serve the hotchpotch with a refreshing salad.

Potato Rösti

(serves 4)

---

4 large potatoes
1 tbsp butter
salt
pepper

1. Peel the potatoes and shred roughly (using a food processor). Squeeze out the shredded potato on to a clean kitchen towel or colander, draining the liquid.
2. Heat the butter in a pan. Put the potatoes in the pan and slightly mash with a fork, creating a cake. Sprinkle with salt and pepper. Fry until the bottom turns golden brown, then turn over and fry the other side until golden brown and serve.

Potato Salad

(serves 1)

---

3 medium-sized
  potatoes
½ onion or shallot
a few chives
1 parsley sprig
¼ celeriac
2 carrots
lamb's lettuce

1. Boil the potatoes in their skins, let them cool, peel and cut into cubes.
2. Peel the onion or shallot and chop.
3. Wash the chives and parsley, pat dry, chop finely and blend with the potato cubes.
4. Peel and roughly shred the celeriac and carrots.
5. Blend the shredded vegetables with the potato cubes and garnish with a few leaves of lettuce.

(See also recipe on p. 26.)

Potatoes with Herb Butter
(serves 4)

1 kg (2 lb 4 oz)
  potatoes
butter with freshly
  chopped herbs

1. Boil the potatoes with or without their skins.
2. Put some herb butter in between the hot potatoes and let the butter melt.
3. Serve with boiled or steamed vegetables.

Potato Salad with Sour Cream
(serves 4)

500 g (18 oz)
  potatoes
1 pepper
2 tbsp sour cream
chives

1. Boil the potatoes in their skins, peel and cut into cubes.
2. Wash the pepper, remove the seeds and mix with the potato cubes. Add the sour cream and garnish with fresh chives.
3. Serve with a salad.

Potato–Celeriac Purée

(serves 4)

---

500 g (18 oz)
  potatoes
300 g (11 oz)
  peeled celeriac
butter
60 ml (⅛ pint;
  ¼ cup) cream
nutmeg
pepper

1. Peel the potatoes and cook with the celeriac.
2. Pour off the water and add the butter and cream.
3. Purée the vegetables and season with nutmeg and pepper.

Herb Purée

(serves 4)

---

mashed potato (see
  recipe on p. 78)
3 tbsp fresh herbs,
  chopped (e.g.
  chives, parsley,
  chervil)

1. To the mashed potato (made from 1 kg of potatoes) add the herbs and blend.
2. Serve with steamed vegetables.

Pasta and Rice Dishes

Fresh Pasta

(serves 2)

200 g (7 oz) durum
  wheat flour
2 eggs
1 tbsp oil

1. Put the flour in a bowl, make a hole in the middle and add the eggs.
2. Add the oil and knead until elastic. Knead the dough into a ball, cover and set aside for 30 minutes.
3. Divide the dough into equal pieces and roll with a rolling pin or use a pasta maker. Cut the dough into strips, slices or other shapes.
4. Cook the pasta until al dente (cooked but not soft).

(The quantities in the following recipes are for dried pasta. If you use fresh pasta for any of the recipes, you will need approximately twice the weight.)

Fine Spaghetti with Mixed Vegetables

(serves 4)

300 g (11 oz) fine
  spaghetti
400 g (14 oz) sugar
  peas
12 baby corncobs
300 g (11 oz)
  mushrooms
3 spring onions
2 tbsp butter
salt
cayenne pepper
creamy red pepper
  sauce (for recipe
  see p. 120)

1. Wash the sugar peas and remove the fibrous threads. Wash the corncobs.
2. Rub the mushrooms clean.
3. Remove the roots and any withered green parts from the spring onions. Slice them.
4. Heat the butter and gently stew the mushrooms, baby corncobs and peas. Season with salt and cayenne pepper.
5. Meanwhile, cook the spaghetti and drain. Divide the spaghetti among 4 preheated plates, together with a few spoons of mixed vegetables and mushrooms. Serve with the creamy red pepper sauce.

Cold Pasta Salad

(serves 1)

100 g (4 oz) mixed pasta
1 broccoli head
a few leaves of iceberg lettuce
1 bundle watercress
2 carrots
2 tbsp mayonnaise (see recipe on p. 114)

1. Cook the pasta until al dente (cooked but not soft) and let it cool.
2. Wash the broccoli and separate into florets. Steam and allow to cool.
3. Wash the lettuce, pat dry and cut into strips.
4. Wash the watercress, pat dry and add to the pasta with the lettuce strips and the broccoli florets.
5. Roughly shred the carrots and mix with the pasta.
6. Add the mayonnaise and mix the salad well.

Pasta with Herbs
(serves 4)

500 g (18 oz) pasta
4 tbsp olive oil
2 tbsp basil or
   parsley, chopped

1. Cook the pasta until al dente (cooked but not soft).
2. Heat the oil and pour over the pasta.
3. Sprinkle with basil or parsley.

Pasta with Steamed Vegetables
(serves 4)

1 small courgette
3 new carrots
300 g (11 oz) fresh
   peas
3 spring onions
400 g (14 oz) pasta
½ onion
1 tbsp butter
250 ml (½ pint;
   1 cup) cream
saffron threads
salt
pepper
fresh thyme

1. Wash the courgette and carrots and cut into equal pieces.
2. Wash the fresh peas and remove any fibrous threads.
3. Wash and remove the roots from the spring onions, cut the green parts into 2 pieces and the onions into 4 pieces.
4. Put the vegetables in a steamer.
5. Meanwhile, cook the pasta until al dente (cooked but not soft) and drain.
6. Peel the onion and sauté in the butter.
7. Add the cream with the saffron threads. Add salt and pepper if required.
8. Pour the cream sauce over the vegetables and serve the pasta and the vegetables in 2 separate bowls.
9. Garnish with thyme.

Three-colour Pasta with Leek Sauce

(serves 4)

3 leeks
200 g (7 oz)
  mushrooms
500–600 g
  (18–21 oz) of
  three-colour pasta
1 tbsp butter
curry powder
pepper
stock granules or
  bouillon powder
250 ml (½ pint;
  1 cup) cream

1. Cut off the roots and any green parts from the leeks (use the green parts for a soup). Cut the leeks in half, wash thoroughly and cut into rings.
2. Rub the mushrooms clean. Remove the lower part of the stalks and slice.
3. Boil the pasta until al dente (cooked but not soft).
4. Meanwhile, heat the butter and stew the leek and the mushrooms. Season with curry powder, pepper and stock granules.
5. Add the cream, stir well and pour over the pasta.
6. Serve with a salad.

Refreshing Pasta Salad

(serves 1)

100 g (4 oz)
  butterfly pasta
1 carrot
1 bundle mustard
  and cress
2 tbsp beansprouts
herb mayonnaise
  (see p. 115 for
  recipe)

1. Boil the pasta until al dente (cooked but not soft) and let it cool.
2. Peel the carrot, shred it and add to the pasta.
3. Wash the mustard and cress and mix with the pasta. Add the beansprouts and mix the salad well.
4. Blend the salad well and coat with the herb mayonnaise.

Tagliatelle with Oyster Mushrooms

(serves 4)

1 kg (2 lb 4 oz)
  oyster mushrooms
1 shallot
1 tbsp butter
1 tbsp olive oil
2 garlic cloves,
  minced
cayenne pepper
400–500 g
  (14–18 oz)
  tagliatelle
250 ml (½ pint;
  1 cup)
  (unsweetened)
  whipped cream
6 fresh basil leaves

1. Rub the mushrooms clean.
2. Peel the shallot and chop finely.
3. Fry the mushrooms and the shallot in butter and olive oil and flavour with garlic and cayenne pepper.
4. Meanwhile, cook the pasta until al dente (cooked but not soft), drain and blend with the mushrooms. Add the cream.
5. Garnish with basil.

Vegetarian Lasagna

(serves 4)

---

450 g (16 oz)
 broccoli
stock granules or
 bouillon powder
salt
pepper
1 endive
2 tbsp butter
200 g (7 oz)
 mushrooms
250 ml (½ pint;
 1 cup) cream
500 g (18 oz)
 lasagna
3 tbsp breadcrumbs

1. Wash the broccoli, divide into florets, cut the stalks into pieces and cook. Purée the broccoli and season with stock granules, salt and pepper.
2. Wash the endive and cook it in the butter. Season.
3. Rub the mushrooms clean, slice and fry in butter.
4. Stir some of the cream into the broccoli purée and some into the endive mixture.
5. Meanwhile, cook the lasagna.
6. Grease a square oven dish and cover the bottom with some of the lasagna strips. Pour a layer of broccoli sauce on to the lasagna. Then put the next layer of lasagna on top, followed by the fried mushrooms, another layer of lasagna and the endive mixture. Continue doing this until the sauces, lasagna and mushrooms have been used up. Make sure the final layer is endive.
7. Sprinkle with breadcrumbs and grill until heated through.

Fried Rice

(to use up left-over boiled rice)

---

boiled rice
1 tbsp oil
garlic
ginger
curry powder

1. Fry the boiled rice briefly in oil and season with garlic, ginger and curry powder.
2. Serve with oriental vegetable dishes.

Nasi Goreng

(serves 4)

---

300 g (11 oz) rice
1 small onion
1 garlic clove
1 large carrot
1 leek
½ red pepper
200 g (7 oz) fresh
 peas
150 g (5 oz)
 mushrooms
1 tbsp oil
1 tbsp soy sauce
½ tsp paprika
¼ tsp curry powder
¼ tsp ginger
fresh chives, chopped

1. Cook the rice.
2. Peel and chop the onion finely and mince the garlic.
3. Peel the carrot and cut finely.
4. Wash the leek and red pepper and cut finely.
5. Cook the peas.
6. Rub the mushrooms clean and slice thinly.
7. Heat the oil in a wok and fry everything together, stirring constantly for 5 minutes.
8. Season with soy sauce. Add the rice and mix with the vegetables. Flavour with paprika, curry powder and ginger.
9. Garnish with chives.

Spicy Pepper Rice

(serves 4)

---

200 g (7 oz) rice
1 red pepper
1 green pepper
½ onion
½ tbsp oil
1 garlic clove,
 minced
2 drops tabasco
½ tsp curry powder

1. Cook the rice.
2. Wash the red and green peppers, remove the seeds and cut finely.
3. Peel the onion and chop finely.
4. Heat the oil and fry the onion and the peppers.
5. Add the garlic and rice. Mix the rice and the vegetables well. Add tabasco and curry powder. Serve as a side-dish.

Risotto with Fungi
(serves 4)

---

250 g (9 oz) rice
1 shallot
1 garlic clove
1 kg (2 lb 4 oz)
  mixed fungi (e.g.
  oyster mushrooms,
  chanterelles,
  Parisian
  mushrooms,
  morels, ceps)
2 tbsp butter
pepper
250 ml (½ pint;
  1 cup) cream
fresh basil leaves
fresh oregano

1. Cook the rice.
2. Peel the shallot and garlic and chop finely.
3. Rub the fungi clean, slice the large ones and leave the small ones whole.
4. Fry the fungi in butter with the shallot and garlic. Season with pepper.
5. Mix the rice with the mixed fungi and add the cream. Season the risotto with basil and oregano.

Mixed Rice
(serves 4)

---

150 g (5 oz) rice
50 g (2 oz) wild rice
1 shallot
1 tbsp butter
paprika
pepper
chives, chopped

1. Cook both types of rice separately.
2. Peel the shallot, shred and fry in butter.
3. Add the rice and season with paprika and pepper.
4. Garnish with chives and serve as a side-dish.

Cold Rice Salad

(serves 4)

---

150 g (5 oz) rice
½ red pepper
1 spring onion
3 tbsp freshly cooked
green peas
3 tbsp cooked
sweetcorn
3 tbsp mayonnaise
(see p. 114 for
recipe)

1. Cook the rice.
2. Wash the pepper, remove the seeds and chop finely.
3. Peel the spring onion, chop finely and blend with the rice and pepper.
4. Mix the peas and sweetcorn with the rice salad. Add the mayonnaise and mix well.
5. Serve with a green salad.

Bread Rolls and Toasts

Raw Vegetable Bread Rolls

(serves 1)

2 bread rolls
2 tbsp mayonnaise
(see p. 114 for recipe)
4 lettuce leaves
¼ cucumber
2 tbsp carrots, shredded
1 bundle mustard and cress
6 radishes
chives, chopped

1. Cut the bread rolls in half and spread with the mayonnaise.
2. Wash the lettuce, pat dry and divide between the bread rolls.
3. Peel the cucumber, slice and put on the bread rolls with the carrots and mustard and cress.
4. Wash the radishes, remove any green parts and slice. Use them to garnish the bread rolls and scatter some finely chopped chives on top.

Avocado Bread Roll

(serves 1)

2 bread rolls
4 lettuce leaves
4 radishes
¼ cucumber
1 bundle mustard and cress
1 avocado
1 tbsp lemon juice
½ tsp curry powder

1. Cut the bread rolls in half.
2. Wash the lettuce, pat dry and cut in strips.
3. Wash the radishes, remove the stalks and slice.
4. Peel the cucumber and slice.
5. Wash the mustard and cress and pat dry.
6. Peel the avocado, cut in half, remove the stone and purée the flesh. Add lemon juice and season with curry powder.
7. Spread the avocado purée on the bread rolls and garnish with the lettuce strips, the radish slices, the cucumber slices and the mustard and cress.

Stuffed Bread Rolls

(serves 1)

2 round bread rolls
2 curly endive leaves
1 piece red cabbage
½–1 tbsp herb
  mayonnaise (see
  p. 114 for recipe)
butter

1. Slice the top off each bread roll, scoop out the contents and cut into cubes.
2. Wash the endive, pat dry, cut finely and put into a bowl.
3. Shred the red cabbage and add to the endive. Add the herb mayonnaise and mix well.

4. Fry the bread cubes in a little butter until golden brown and add to the salad.
5. Fill the bread rolls with the salad.

Mushroom Toast

(serves 4)

---

4 slices bread
200 g (7 oz)
  mushrooms
1 tbsp butter
125 ml (¼ pint;
  ½ cup) cream
  sauce (for recipe
  see p. 121)
nutmeg
paprika
stock granules or
  bouillon powder
pepper
2 tbsp breadcrumbs

1. Toast the bread.
2. Rub the mushrooms clean and slice.
3. Heat the butter and stew the mushrooms.
4. Stir in the mushrooms into the cream sauce and season with nutmeg, paprika, stock granules and pepper. Add some cornflour paste (cornflour mixed with water) to the sauce to thicken if necessary.
5. Spread a thick layer of the mushroom sauce over the toasted bread and sprinkle with the breadcrumbs.
6. Put the toasted bread under the grill until brown. Arrange on plates, decorated with raw vegetables.

Toast with Scrambled Eggs

(serves 4)

---

4 slices bread
4 egg yolks
4 tbsp water
salt
pepper
1 parsley sprig
4 chive blades
2 basil leaves
4 oregano leaves
1 tbsp butter

1. Toast the bread.
2. Beat the egg yolks and water in a bowl and add salt and pepper.
3. Finely chop the herbs and stir into the beaten eggs.
4. Melt the butter in a pan, add the eggs and let them set while stirring.
5. Put the scrambled eggs on the toasted bread and arrange on 4 plates.

Stuffed Bread Rolls with Leek Ragoût

(serves 4)

4 round crusty bread rolls
1 leek
150 g (5 oz) mushrooms
6 cooked asparagus spears
2 tbsp butter
125 ml (¼ pint; ½ cup) (unsweetened) whipped cream
pepper
stock granules or bouillon powder

1. Slice the top off each bread roll, scoop out the contents and cut into cubes to fry afterwards in some of the butter (croûtons).
2. Grill the bread rolls briefly until crusty.
3. Clean the leek, discarding any roots and green parts and cut into rings.
4. Rub the mushrooms clean and slice.
5. Cut the asparagus into pieces.
6. Heat the rest of the butter and stew the leek rings and the mushroom slices. Add the asparagus pieces.
7. Mix with the cream and season with pepper and stock granules.
8. Fill the toasted rolls with the ragoût, sprinkle them with the croûtons and serve with raw vegetables and any remaining sauce.

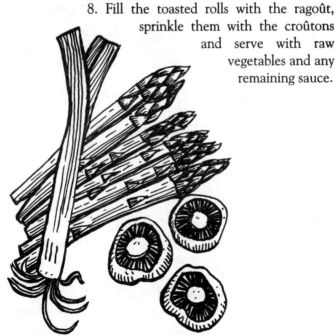

Spicy Bread Croûtons
(serves 4)

2 slices bread
1 tbsp butter
1 tbsp olive oil
1 garlic clove, minced
2 tbsp fresh herbs, chopped

1. Remove the crusts from the bread, discard and cut the bread into cubes.
2. Heat the butter and olive oil and fry the bread cubes until crusty.
3. Add the garlic and herbs.
4. Serve these croûtons with a salad or soup.

Bread Rolls with Fried Pepper
(serves 2)

2 bread rolls
1 red pepper
1 tbsp oil
1 garlic clove, minced
2 curly endive leaves

1. Cut the bread rolls in half.
2. Wash the pepper, remove the seeds and cut into strips.
3. Heat the oil and fry the pepper strips with the garlic.
4. Put the endive on the bread rolls, together with the pepper strips.

Oyster Mushroom Buns

(serves 2)

2 round bread rolls
200 g (7 oz) oyster
  mushrooms
1 tbsp butter
1 garlic clove,
  minced
2 lettuce leaves
1 tbsp mayonnaise
  (see p. 114 for
  recipe)
1 tbsp (unsweetened)
  whipped cream
fresh herbs
salt
pepper

1. Cut the bread rolls in half.
2. Rub the mushrooms clean and fry in butter with the garlic.
3. Put the lettuce and mushrooms on the rolls.
4. Mix the mayonnaise with the cream, herbs, salt and pepper.
5. Put a spoonful of this sauce on each bread roll.

Cheese Dishes

Cheese Salad

(serves 1)

---

100 g (3.5 oz)
  cheese (e.g.
  vegetarian cheese,
  camembert, gouda,
  brie)
mixed lettuce
4 lamb's lettuce
  florets
1 tomato
1 chicory spear
chives
radish
100 g (3.5 oz) fresh
  low-fat soft cheese
fresh herbs, chopped

1. Wash the mixed and lamb's lettuces and pat dry.
2. Wash the tomato and cut into pieces.
3. Cut the chicory in half, remove the bitter core and cut finely.
4. Mix the vegetables together and garnish with chives and the radish.
5. Serve with the cheese, accompanied by a dressing of soft cheese mixed with herbs.

Stuffed Mushrooms

(serves 4)

---

20 medium-sized
  mushrooms
200 g (7 oz) quark
1 tbsp cheese, grated
1 garlic clove,
  minced
parsley
chives
2 basil leaves
pepper
paprika

1. Rub the mushrooms clean, remove the stalks and set aside for another dish.
2. Blend the quark with the cheese and garlic. Season this mixture with the finely chopped herbs, pepper and paprika.
3. Fill the mushroom buttons with the quark mixture and place under the grill until brown.

(You could also use small tomatoes instead of the mushrooms. An alternative recipe for Stuffed Mushrooms appears on p. 2.)

Fruity Cheese Sticks

(snack or appetizer for 4)

4 pieces cheese of
your choice
(camembert,
gouda, brie,
cheddar)
2 kiwi fruit
1 bunch black
grapes
2 mandarin oranges
8 skewers

1. Cut the cheese into equal cubes.
2. Peel the kiwi fruit and cut into cubes.
3. Wash the grapes and remove from their stems.
4. Peel the mandarin oranges and separate into segments.
5. Arrange cheese and fruit cubes alternately on the skewers.

Mushrooms in Boursin
(serves 4)

---

500 g (18 oz)
  mushrooms
1 tbsp butter
1 packet Boursin
1 garlic clove,
  minced

1. Rub the mushrooms clean and slice thinly.
2. Stew the mushrooms in butter. Add the Boursin (or another herb cream cheese) and garlic. Heat until the cheese has melted.
3. Serve with a salad.

Stuffed Cherry Tomatoes
(serves 4)

12 or 16 cherry
  tomatoes
150 g (5 oz) cream
  cheese
chives
celery salt
mustard and cress
a few lettuce leaves

1. Wash and dry the tomatoes. Cut off the tops and scoop out the flesh using a sharp knife.
2. Mix the cream cheese with the finely chopped chives and celery salt.
3. Fill the tomatoes with this mixture and garnish the plate with mustard and cress and lettuce.

Tomatoes Covered with Cheese

(serves 4)

---

5 tomatoes
2 mozzarella
 cheeses
salt
pepper
5 basil leaves

1. Wash the tomatoes, dry, remove the stalks and slice.
2. Slice the mozzarella cheese (using an egg slicer).
3. Put the cheese and tomato slices alternately into a greased oven dish. Sprinkle with some salt and pepper and grill until the cheese has melted.
4. Wash the basil, pat dry, cut finely and scatter over the hot dish.

Stuffed Fennel Roots

(serves 2 to 3)

---

4 large fennel roots
½ red pepper
1 shallot
1 tbsp butter
1 garlic clove,
 minced
gruyère cheese,
 grated

1. Wash the fennel, remove the brown spots and steam. Use a teaspoon to make a hole in the roots and then cut the scooped out flesh into pieces.
2. Wash the pepper, remove the seeds and cut the flesh into pieces.
3. Peel the shallot and chop finely.
4. Heat the butter and stew the pepper, the onion and the fennel. Season with garlic.
5. Fill the fennel roots with the vegetable mixture and sprinkle some cheese on top. Grill until the cheese has melted.

Stuffed Goat's Cheese

(appetizer for 4)

---

4 fresh goat's
cheeses (75 g,
3 oz each)
150 g (5 oz) cream
cheese
1 tbsp fresh basil
leaves, chopped
1 parsley sprig,
chopped
3 chives
watercress

1. Cut the goat's cheeses in half horizontally.
2. Mix the cream cheese with the basil, parsley and chives.
3. Spread the cream cheese mixture over 4 of the goat's cheese halves. Put the remaining halves on top. Garnish with a bed of watercress.

Goat's Cheese au Gratin

(appetizer for 4)

---

4 goat's cheeses
curly endive
lamb's lettuce
tomato
cucumber

1. Grill the goat's cheeses briefly.
2. Serve them on a bed of endive, lamb's lettuce, tomato and cucumber.

Pear with Goat's Cheese

(appetizer for 4)

---

2 pears
150 g (5 oz) goat's
cheese
100 g (3.5 oz)
cream cheese
pepper
4 mint leaves

1. Peel the pears, remove the cores, slice and arrange on 4 plates.
2. Cut off the rind from the goat's cheese, flatten the cheese with a fork, stir in the cream cheese and season with pepper.

3. With cool hands, roll the cheese into a sausage shape, and cut into 12 equal slices.
4. Divide the cheese slices among the 4 plates and garnish with mint.

Gorgonzola Mushrooms

(serves 4)

250 g (9 oz) mushrooms
150 g (5 oz) gorgonzola
fresh chives

1. Rub the mushrooms clean, remove the stalks and set them aside for another dish.

2. Flatten the gorgonzola with a fork and fill the mushroom buttons with it.
3. Put the mushroom buttons on to a greased oven dish, sprinkle with some finely shredded chives and grill until the cheese has melted.

Cheese Dish

(serves 4)

1 piece brie
1 piece camembert
1 piece herb cheese
1 piece gouda, etc
3 bunches of grapes
2 mandarin oranges
2 kiwi fruit
3 apricots

1. Arrange the cheeses on a large cheese-board.
2. Garnish with the fruit.

Quark with Forest-Fruits

(serves 4)

150 g (5 oz) forest-fruits (raspberries, blackberries, redcurrants ...)
200 g (7 oz) low-fat quark
4 tbsp whipped cream

1. Wash and dry the forest-fruits.
2. Mix the quark with the forest-fruits and decorate with the cream.
3. Garnish with left-over fruits if required.

Cheese–Fruit Salad

(serves 4)

150 g (5 oz) young edam or gouda
1 orange
1 kiwi fruit
1 orange
1 apple

1. Remove the rind from the cheese and cut the cheese into cubes.
2. Peel the orange and separate into segments.
3. Peel the kiwi fruit, cut into pieces and mix with the cheese and orange.
4. Peel the apple, remove the core, cut into pieces and mix with the salad.

Dressings and Sauces

Mayonnaise

1 egg
1 tsp mustard
½ tsp oil (preferably
  not olive oil)
1 or 2 lemons
salt
pepper

1. In a blender mix together the egg and the mustard.
2. Add the oil little by little. Add the lemon juice and season with salt and pepper.
(If you want to beat the mayonnaise by hand, only use the egg yolk.)

Vinaigrette

1 tsp mustard or
  mustard seed,
  ground
125 ml (¼ pint;
  ½ cup) oil
60 ml (⅛ pint; ¼ cup)
  wine vinegar, cider
  vinegar or lemon
  juice
spices
herbs
½ onion

1. Mix the mustard with the oil and vinegar.
2. Season with spices, herbs and finely chopped onion.

Tomato Vinaigrette

1 cup vinaigrette
  (without onion) (see
  above for recipe)
2 tbsp tomato
  ketchup
oregano
paprika

1. Mix the vinaigrette with the tomato ketchup.
2. Season with oregano and paprika.

Yoghurt Dressing

2 parts mayonnaise
  (see previous page
  for recipe)
1 part yoghurt or
  buttermilk
fresh or dried herbs,
  chopped
onion
garlic

1. Blend the mayonnaise with the yoghurt or buttermilk.
2. Season with the herbs, onion and garlic.

Herb Mayonnaise

2 tbsp mayonnaise
  (see previous page
  for recipe)
1 tbsp fresh herbs

Blend the mayonnaise with the fresh herbs.

Sour Cream

200 g (7 oz) sour
 cream
fresh garden herbs
 (e.g. dill, chives,
 parsley, basil,
 peppermint)

Mix the sour cream with the herbs.

Spicy Red Sauce

125 ml (¼ pint;
 ½ cup) tomato
 ketchup
1 tbsp horseradish
 paste
1 tsp French mustard
½ tbsp white wine
 vinegar
½ tbsp lemon juice
3 drops tabasco
1 spring onion
cayenne pepper
paprika

1. Mix the tomato ketchup, horseradish, mustard, vinegar, lemon juice and tabasco together.
2. Finely cut the spring onion and add to the rest. Blend the sauce well and season with cayenne pepper and paprika.

3. Serve with iceberg lettuce and grilled vegetables.

Mustard Sauce

3 tbsp mustard (with seeds)
2 tbsp mayonnaise (see p. 114 for recipe)
1 tbsp lemon juice
2 tbsp sour cream
2 lemon balm leaves

1. Mix the mustard, mayonnaise, lemon juice and sour cream together.
2. Finely cut the lemon balm and add to the sauce.
3. Serve with boiled or steamed asparagus.

Louisiana Salad Dressing

3 tbsp home-made aïoli (see next page for recipe)
2 tbsp sour cream
2 tbsp tomato ketchup
1 tsp lemon juice
1 tsp spicy mustard
2 spring onions
cayenne pepper
2 drops tabasco
horseradish
salt

1. Mix the aïoli (garlic mayonnaise) with the sour cream, tomato ketchup, lemon juice and mustard.
2. Clean the onions, chop finely and mix with the dressing.
3. Season with cayenne pepper, tabasco, horseradish and salt.
4. Refrigerate for a few hours, before serving with a mixed salad.

Aïoli (garlic mayonnaise)

1 tsp mustard
1 egg yolk
250 ml (½ pint;
  1 cup) olive oil
½ lemon
2 garlic cloves

1. Prepare a mayonnaise consisting of mustard, egg yolk and olive oil.
2. Add the juice of half a lemon.
3. Squeeze the juice from the garlic over the mayonnaise.
4. Serve with cold potatoes or as a dip.

Cocktail Sauce

4 tbsp mayonnaise
(see p. 114 for
recipe)
2 tbsp tomato
ketchup
1 tsp paprika
pepper

1. Mix the mayonnaise with the tomato ketchup and paprika. Season with pepper.
2. Serve with salads, as a dip or with cold stuffed tomatoes.

Diet Dressing

4 beefsteak tomatoes
½ tbsp lemon juice
pepper
fresh basil
oregano

1. Skin the tomatoes, cut into pieces, purée and drain.
2. Mix the tomato purée with lemon juice.
3. Season with pepper, basil and oregano.

Istanbul Garlic Sauce

4 tbsp mayonnaise
(see p. 114 for
recipe)
2 tbsp Greek yoghurt
¼ cucumber
2 garlic cloves
salt
pepper
1 tbsp chives,
chopped

1. Mix the mayonnaise with the yoghurt.
2. Peel the cucumber, shred and add to the sauce.
3. Peel the garlic and squeeze the juice on to the cucumber.
4. Season with salt and pepper and garnish with chives.

Creamy Red Pepper Sauce

1 tbsp butter or
  margarine
2 red peppers
125 ml (¼ pint;
  ½ cup) cream
1 shallot
pepper
salt

1. Chop the peppers and the shallot finely.
2. Fry the peppers and shallot in the butter or margarine until soft.
3. Put the vegetables into a blender together with the cream and season with salt and pepper.
4. Blend until smooth and serve hot.

Mexican Avocado Dip

2 ripe avocados
3 tbsp lime juice
1 tomato, skinned
  and deseeded
1 shallot, finely
  chopped
pepper
tabasco

1. Peel the avocados, remove the stones and cut into pieces.
2. Add the lime juice, tomato and shallot.
3. Purée the ingredients until the sauce becomes smooth. Season with pepper and tabasco and serve as a dip with vegetables and tortillas.

Curry Sauce

½ onion
butter
1 tsp curry powder
250 ml (½ pint;
  1 cup) vegetable
  stock (see p. 10 for
  recipe)
cornflour
water
pepper
paprika
saffron

1. Peel the onion, cut finely and sauté in the butter.
2. Add the curry powder, stirring constantly to prevent burning and then add the stock.
3. Let the sauce heat through and thicken with the cornflour mixed with a little water.
4. Season with pepper, paprika and saffron.

Sauce Provençal

½ onion
½ pepper
1 tbsp olive oil
3 beefsteak tomatoes
2 bay leaves
1 pinch oregano
1 pinch basil
1 pinch mixed herbs
1 tsp stock granules
  or bouillon powder
paprika
pepper

1. Peel the onion and cut finely.
2. Wash the pepper, remove the seeds and cut finely.
3. Heat the olive oil and stew the onion and the pepper.
4. Remove the seeds from the tomatoes, skin them and add to the pepper.
5. Add the herbs and stock granules.
6. Simmer on a low heat and season with paprika and pepper.

Cream Sauce

1 oz (25 g) butter or
  margarine
1 tbsp of flour
125 ml (¼ pint;
  ½ cup) vegetable
  stock
125 ml (¼ pint;
  ½ cup) cream
nutmeg
salt
pepper
paprika

1. Heat the butter or margarine until it has melted.
2. Add the flour while stirring constantly.
3. Add the vegetable stock while stirring until the sauce has thickened.
4. Add the cream and season with nutmeg, salt, pepper and paprika.

Cheese Sauce

As recipe for Cream Sauce, but instead of cream use 100 g (3.5 oz) of grated cheese such as cheddar, emmental or gruyère.

Tomato Sauce

½ onion
4 beefsteak tomatoes
1 tbsp oil
pepper
stock granules or
  bouillon powder
fresh basil

1. Peel the onion and cut finely.
2. Cut the tomatoes into pieces.
3. Heat the oil and stew the onion and the tomato. Purée the sauce and strain.
4. Season with pepper, stock granules and basil.

Broccoli Sauce

200 g (7 oz) broccoli
125 ml (¼ pint;
  ½ cup) cream
pepper
stock granules or
  bouillon powder

1. Wash the broccoli, cut into pieces and steam.
2. Purée the broccoli.
3. Add the cream and season with pepper and stock granules.

Non-alcoholic Beverages

Orange–Ginger Drink

10 oranges
1 grapefruit
½ tsp ginger or fresh ginger, shredded

1. Squeeze the oranges and grapefruit.
2. Add the ginger.
3. Pour the juice into tall glasses and serve.

Melon Bowl

1 medium-sized honeydew melon
¾ litre (1½ pints; 3 cups) water
1 lemon
1 whole cinnamon stick
4 mint leaves
1 tbsp honey

1. Peel the melon, remove the seeds, cut into cubes and put in a large bowl.
2. Boil the water, adding the juice of the lemon, the cinnamon and the mint. Also add honey if required.
3. Pour the warm mixture over the melon and let it cool.

Moroccan Peppermint Tea

½ litre (1 pint; 2 cups)
  boiling water
1 handful fresh
  peppermint leaves
1 tea bag mint tea
2 tbsp honey

1. Pour the boiling water over the peppermint leaves and tea bag.
2. Leave the tea for a while and then add the honey.

(A refreshing tea for a hot summer day.)

Yoghurt Drink

150 g (5 oz)
  raspberries
½ litre (1 pint; 2 cups)
  yoghurt
whipped cream

1. Purée the raspberries.
2. Drain and mix with the yoghurt.
3. Divide among 4 glasses and use a piping bag to decorate with cream.

Banana Drink

2 bananas
250 ml (½ pint;
  1 cup) yoghurt
125 ml (¼ pint;
  ½ cup) cream

1. Peel and purée the bananas.
2. Add the yoghurt and cream.
3. Put in a blender until creamy.

Apricot Milk

6 apricots, dried
½ litre (1 pint; 2 cups)
  buttermilk

1. Soak the apricots in water, cut into pieces and add the buttermilk and a tablespoon of the liquid from the apricots.
2. Blend the mixture until creamy.

Hibiscus Punch

½ litre (1 pint; 2 cups) boiling water
2 tea bags or hibiscus tea
½ litre (1 pint; 2 cups) apple juice
whipped cream
cinnamon

1. Pour the boiling water over the tea bags. Leave the tea for 5 minutes.
2. Remove the tea bags from the water and add the apple juice.
3. Heat the liquid again and pour into cups.
4. Add some cream to each cup and sprinkle with cinnamon.

Rose Hip–Orange Tea

2 tea bags rose hip tea
1 tea bag orange blossom tea
½ litre (1 pint; 2 cups) boiling water
½ orange
honey

1. Leave the tea in the boiling water for a while.
2. Wash the orange and slice. Divide the slices among 4 cups and pour the tea over.
3. Sweeten with honey if necessary.

Refreshing Summer Punch

100 g (3.5 oz)
  forest-fruits
  (raspberries,
  blackberries,
  redcurrants ...)
4 tbsp crushed ice
freshly squeezed
  orange juice

1. Wash, purée and sieve the forest-fruits.
2. Divide between 4 glasses.
3. Sprinkle the crushed ice on top.
4. Top up with the fresh orange juice.

Examples of Menus

... for elaborate dining

Stuffed mushrooms
Raw vegetable soup
Steamed vegetables

Southern tomatoes
Gazpacho
Gardener's salad

Avocado stuffed with raw
vegetables
Creamy cucumber soup
Steamed vegetables

Garlic tomatoes
Corn–cheese salad
Ratatouille

Oyster mushrooms coated with
breadcrumbs
Leek soup
Refreshing pasta salad

Fennel au gratin
Raw tomato soup
Aubergine with tomatoes from
the oven

Avocado dip
Mushroom soup
Fine spaghetti with mixed
vegetables

Cauliflower soup
Potato salad
Green salad

Creamy asparagus soup
Creamy Brussels sprouts with
carrot
Potatoes

Raw vegetables with dips
Festive cream soup
Potato puffs with steamed
vegetables

Celeriac soup
Steamed cauliflower with herb
dressing
Potatoes

Avocado soup
Fried vegetables
Rice

Pumpkin soup
Stuffed cabbage rolls with
Spicy rice

Chinese vegetable soup
Mixed vegetables from the wok
Nasi Goreng

Fine herb cream soup
Fine asparagus salad
Vegetable tagliatelle with
coriander sauce

... for quick dining

Clear vegetable soup
Spicy mushroom slices

Stuffed artichoke
Spicy tomato salad

Onion soup
Tasty croissants

Minestrone
Stuffed tomatoes from warmer
regions

Artichoke soup
Steamed vegetables

Minestrone (without cheese)
Raw vegetable bread roll

Avocado soup
Bread with leek ragoût

... for fruit lovers

Fruity cheese sticks
Stuffed pineapple (without
cream)

Stuffed pear on a bed of
strawberries
Winter pineapple

Cinnamon apples
Stuffed pineapple (without
cream)

Citrus salad
Layers of fruit salad

Stuffed apricots
Summer fruit with forest-fruit
sauce

Avocado mousse
Fruit salad

Blanched pears with marjoram
Pineapple salad with coconut

Recipe Index

Appetizers

Soups

Salads

Fruit Preparations

Warm Dishes

Potato Dishes

Pasta and Rice Dishes

Bread Rolls and Toasts

Cheese Dishes

Dressings and Sauces

Non-alcoholic Beverages